KAKOOMA®

MULTIPLICATION EDITION

Created by Greg Tang

SCHOLASTIC INC.
NEW YORK TORONTO LONDON AUCKLAND
SYDNEY MEXICO CITY NEW DELHI HONG KONG

TO GREG, EMILY AND KATIE

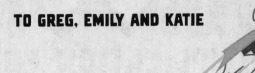

Character design by Michaela Zanzani
Illustrated by Bill Alger

12 11 10 9 8 7 6 5 4 3 2 12 13 14 15 16

ISBN 978-0-545-46755-1
Printed in the U.S.A. 40
First printing, March 2012

TABLE OF CONTENTS

WHAT IS KAKOOMA?

Kakooma starts with a deceptively simple idea: In a group of numbers, find the number that is the sum or product of two others. Sounds easy, right? Sometimes it is, but other times the answer is right in front of you and you just can't see it. To solve a single puzzle, you often end up doing dozens of calculations in your head. Before you know it, your mind is sharper and your math skills are better. Kakooma makes you smarter.

WHO INVENTED KAKOOMA?

Meet Greg Tang. For the past 10 years, Greg Tang has traveled across the United States doing more than 1,300 conferences, workshops, and school visits. Along the way, he has taught more than 250,000 children and adults, helped write several math textbooks, authored eight children's books including a *NY Times* best-seller, and created a family of innovative math puzzles and games.

Greg believes that to be good in math, children need to learn to think abstractly at an early age. When kids learn to think abstractly and efficiently about numbers in groups rather than counting or memorizing, they can be taught common-sense strategies that make calculations fast and easy. Being able to connect and generalize these strategies across problems and operations is the key to thinking algebraically and the secret to being math smart.

HOW TO PLAY KAKOOMA

The Kakooma game board includes several different mini-puzzles (the diagram below shows five mini-puzzles with five numbers in each puzzle). In each mini-puzzle, there is only one number out of the five that is the product of two others. Circle that number—that's your answer. Use all five answers to create the final "puzzle-in-a-puzzle." The answer in the final puzzle is the number that is the sum of two others. Here's an example:

Choose a mini-puzzle to start with. Since 5 x 8 = 40, the answer is 40.

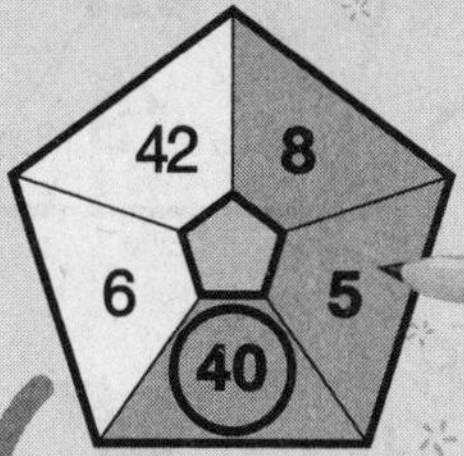

Next, look at the mini-puzzle to the right. Since 6 x 4 = 24, the answer is 24. Solve the three remaining mini-puzzles the same way and all five products form . . . another puzzle!

In this final puzzle, solve for the answer using addition. Find the number that is the sum of two others. Here, the final answer is 24 + 16 = 40.

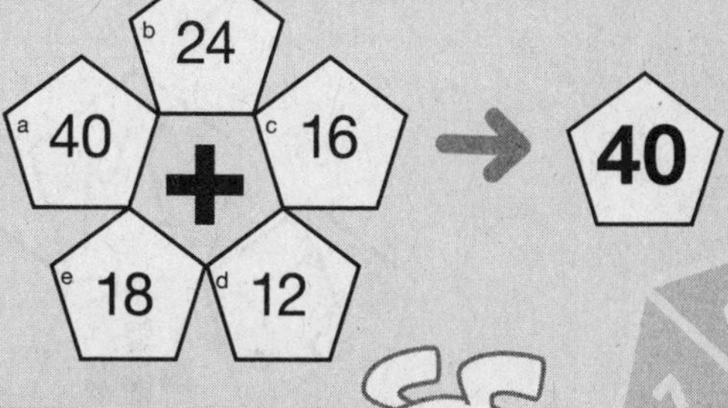

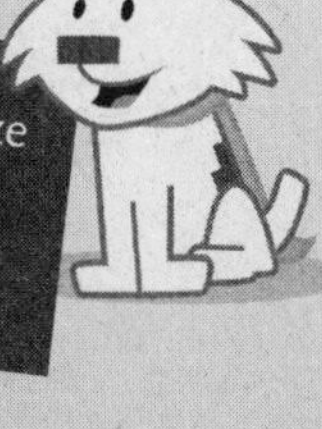

Difficulty levels The size of the puzzle and the size of the puzzle's numbers determine its difficulty. This book starts with the simplest "easy 5" puzzles and then progresses on to more difficult levels.

KAKOOMA EASY 5 MULTIPLICATION

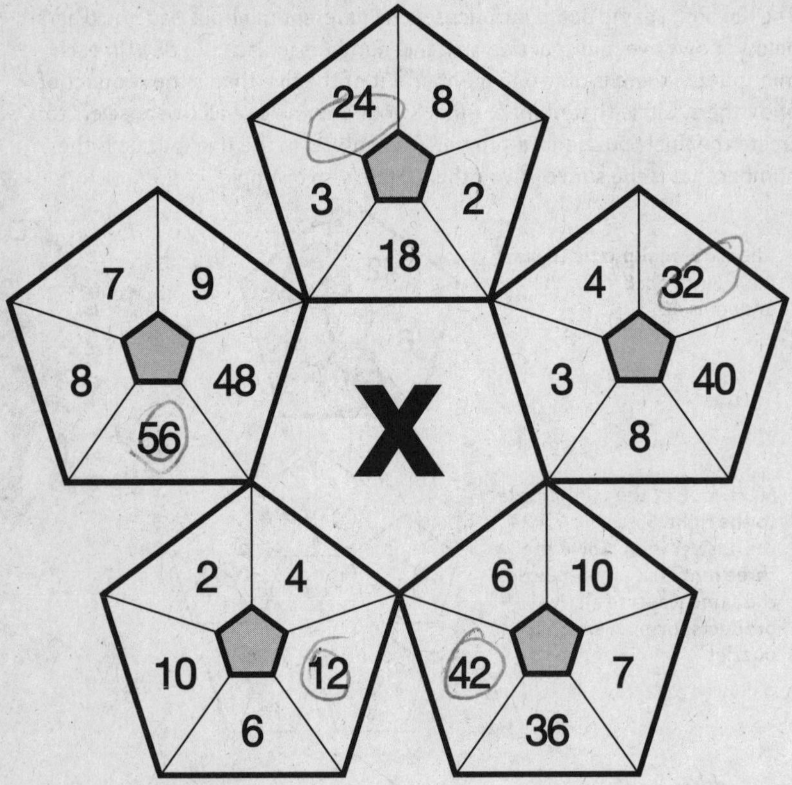

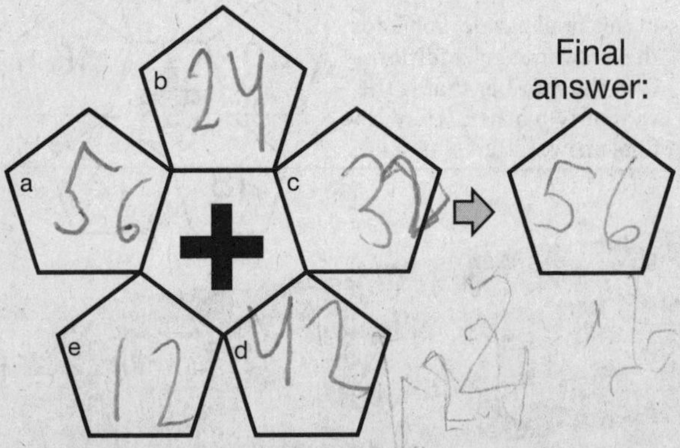

KAKOOMA EASY 5 MULTIPLICATION

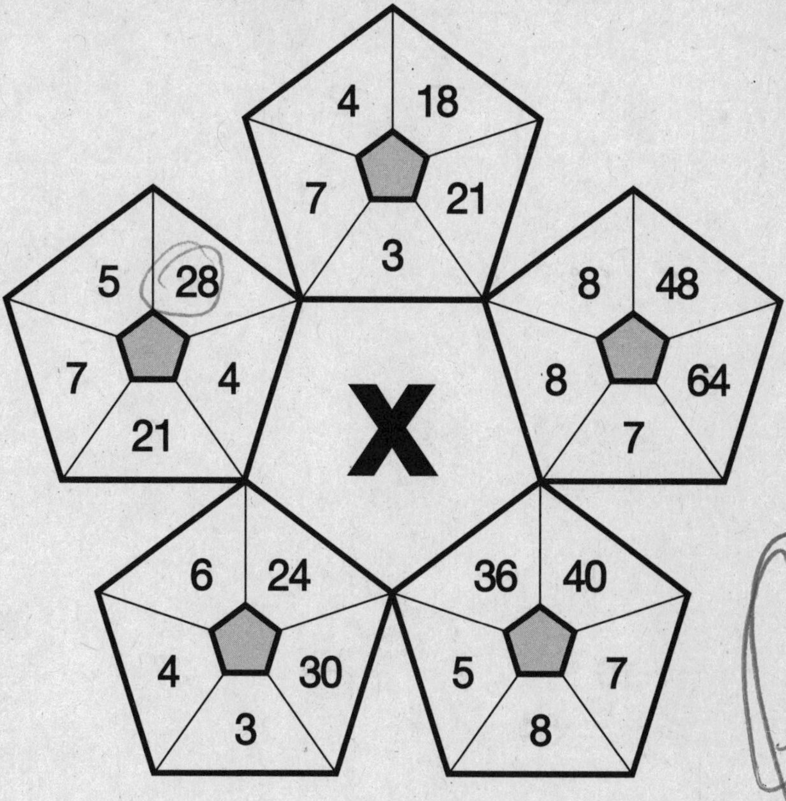

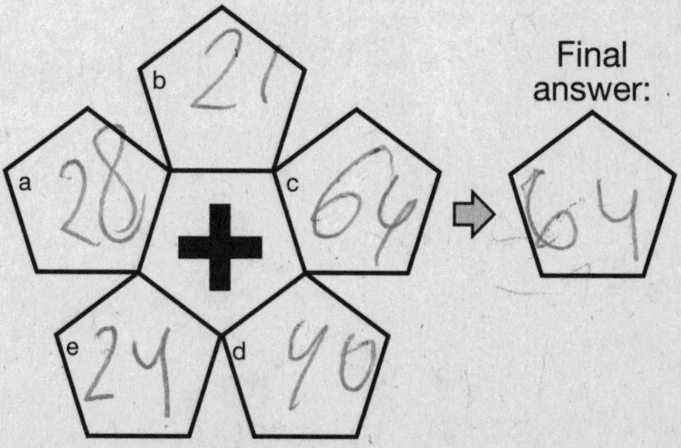

KAKOOMA EASY 5 MULTIPLICATION

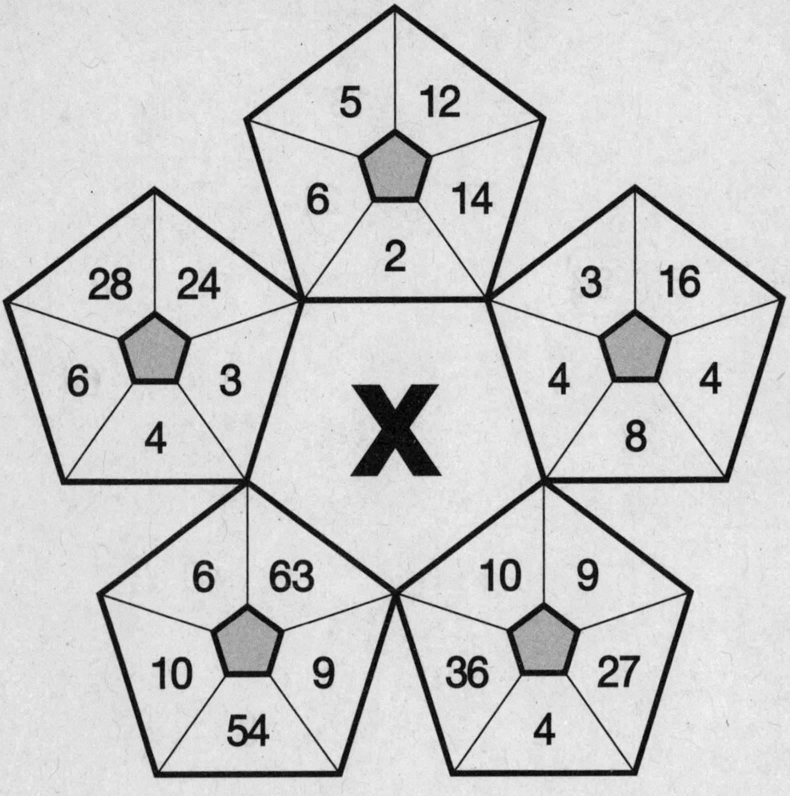

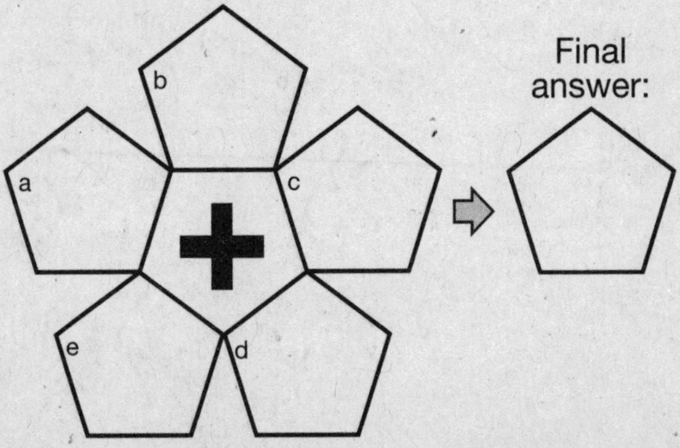

KAKOOMA EASY 5 MULTIPLICATION

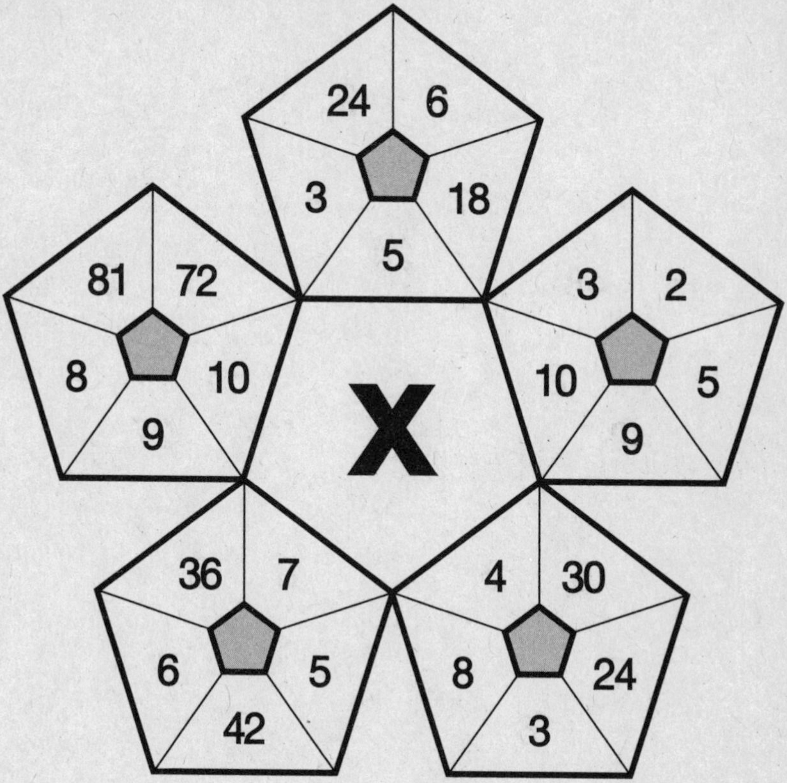

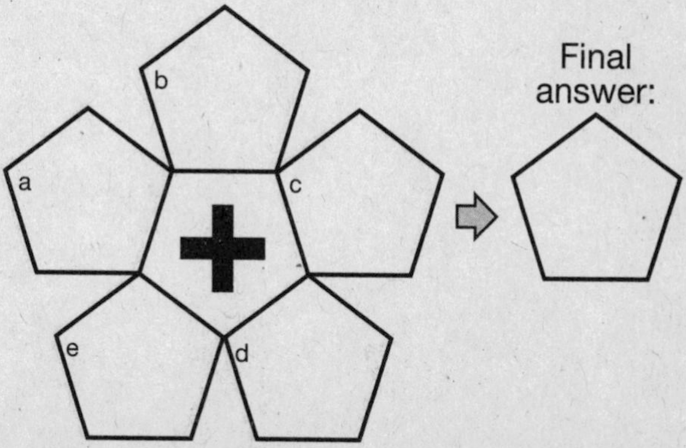

KAKOOMA EASY 5 MULTIPLICATION

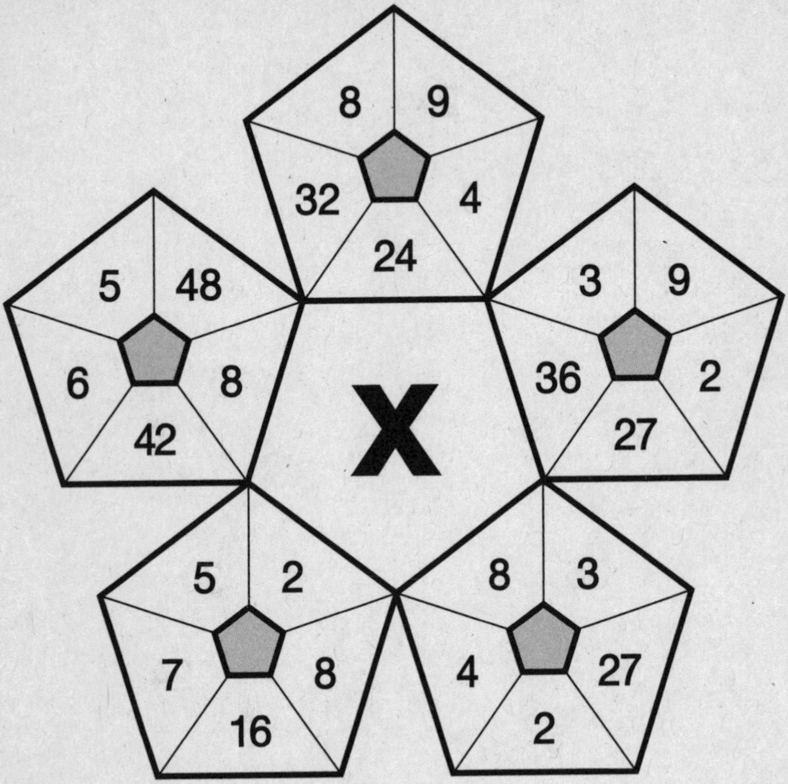

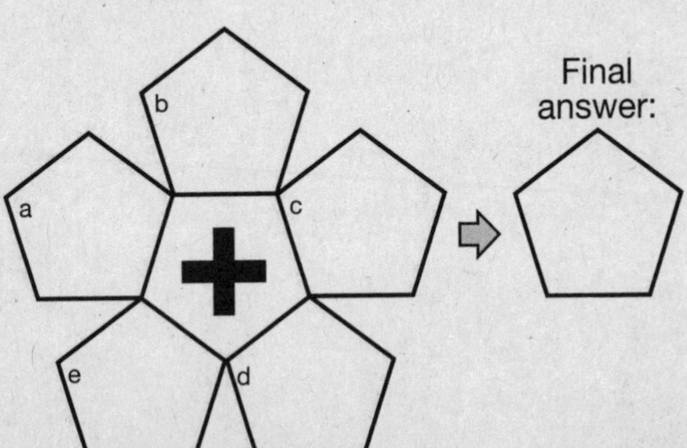

KAKOOMA EASY 5 MULTIPLICATION

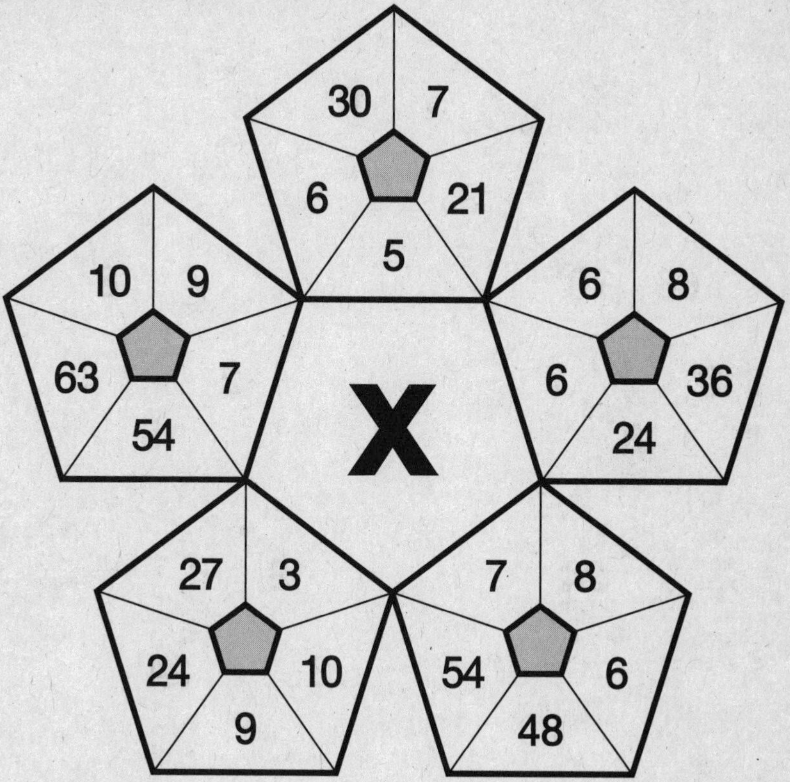

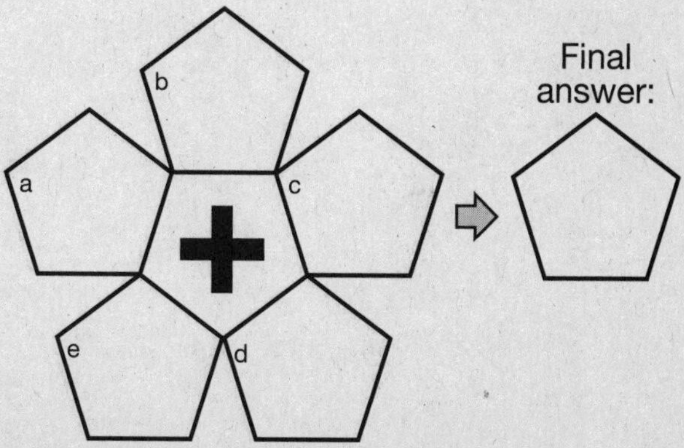

KAKOOMA EASY 5 MULTIPLICATION

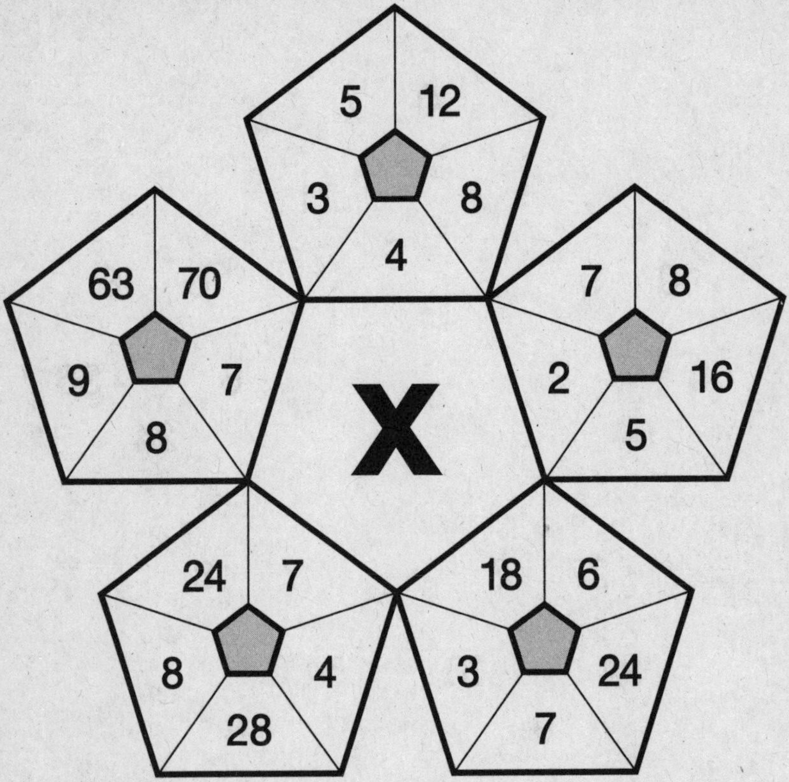

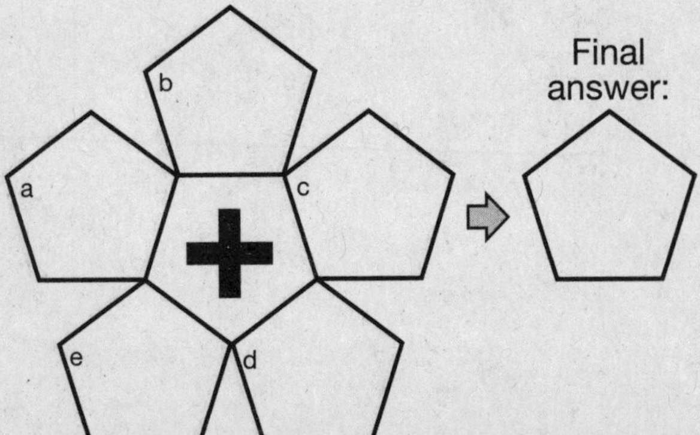

KAKOOMA EASY 5 MULTIPLICATION

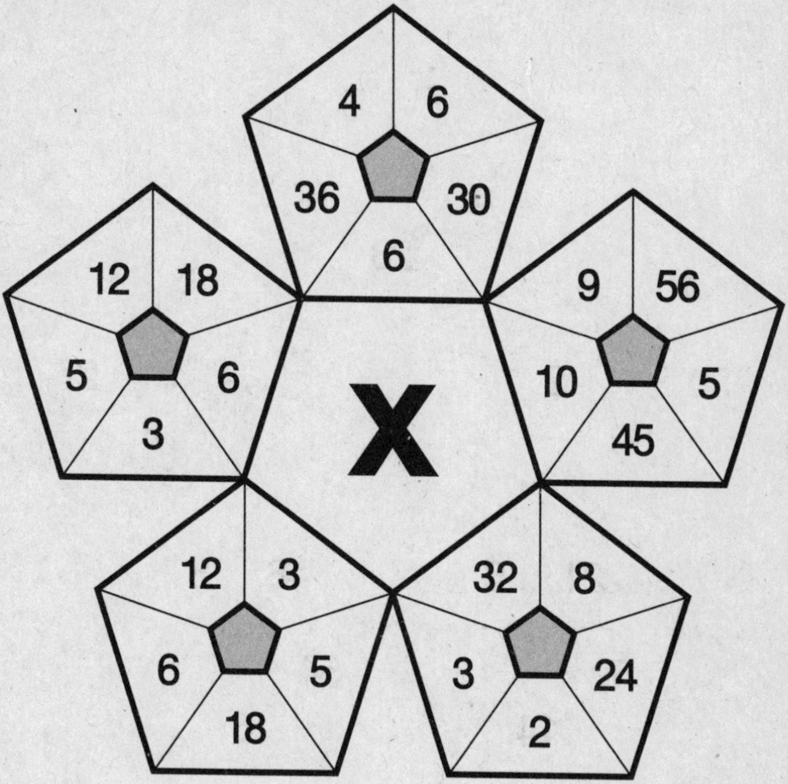

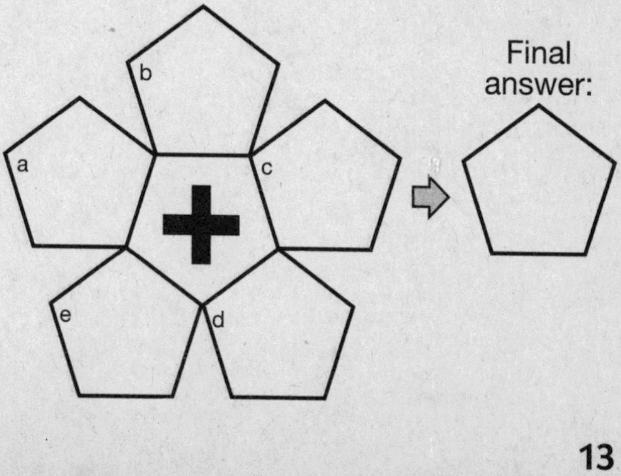

KAKOOMA EASY 5 MULTIPLICATION

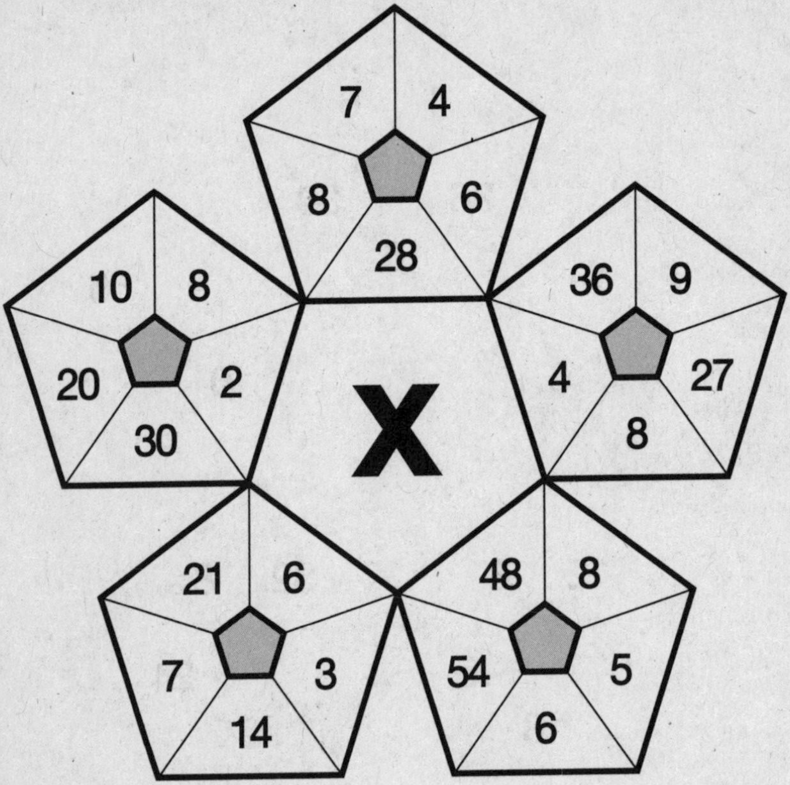

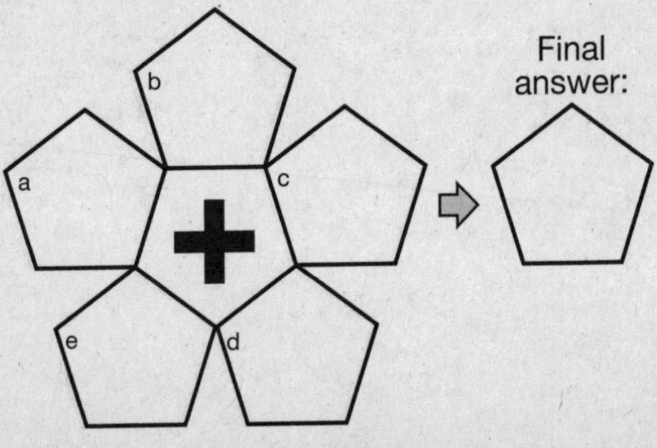

KAKOOMA EASY 5 MULTIPLICATION

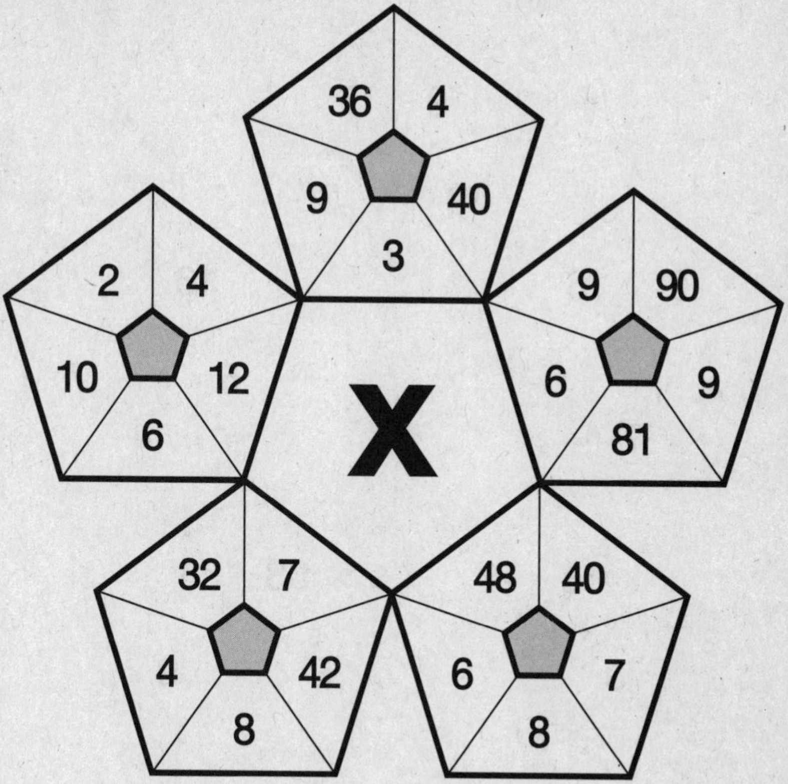

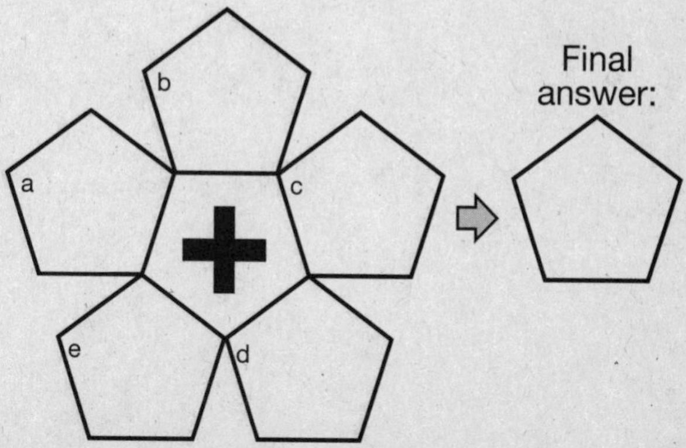

KAKOOMA EASY 5 MULTIPLICATION

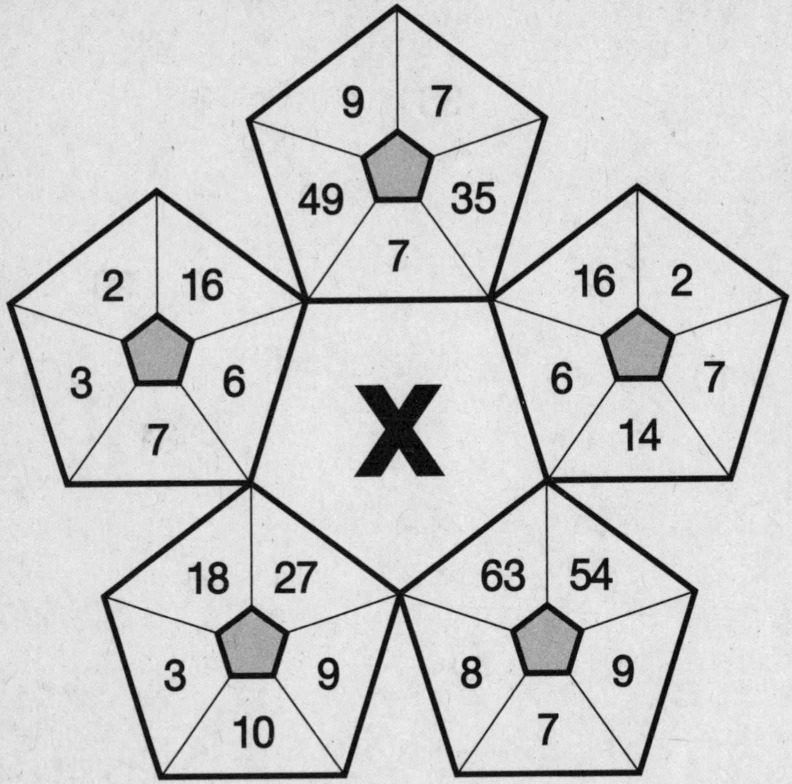

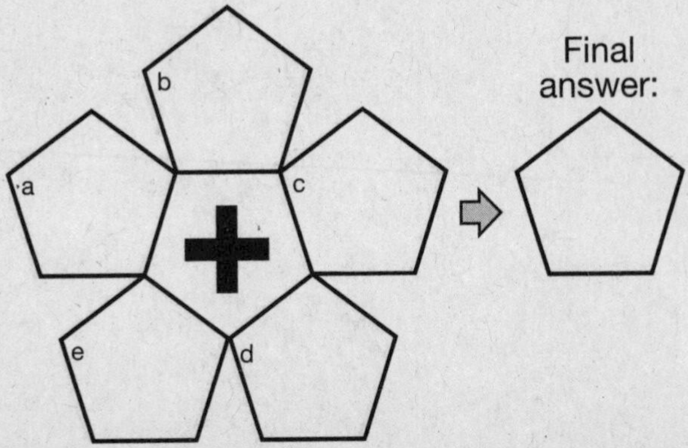

KAKOOMA EASY 5 MULTIPLICATION

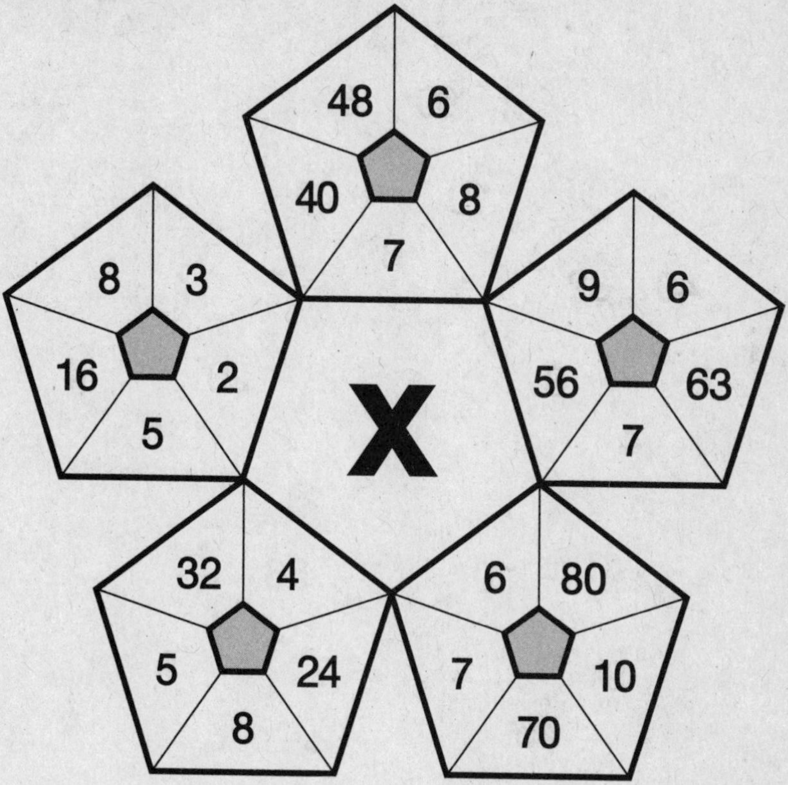

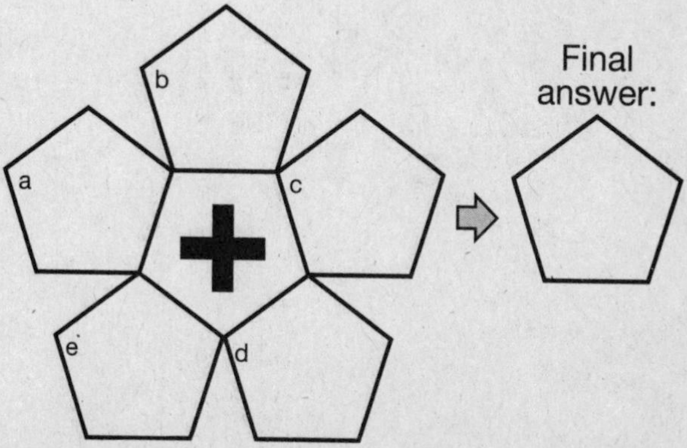

KAKOOMA EASY 5 MULTIPLICATION

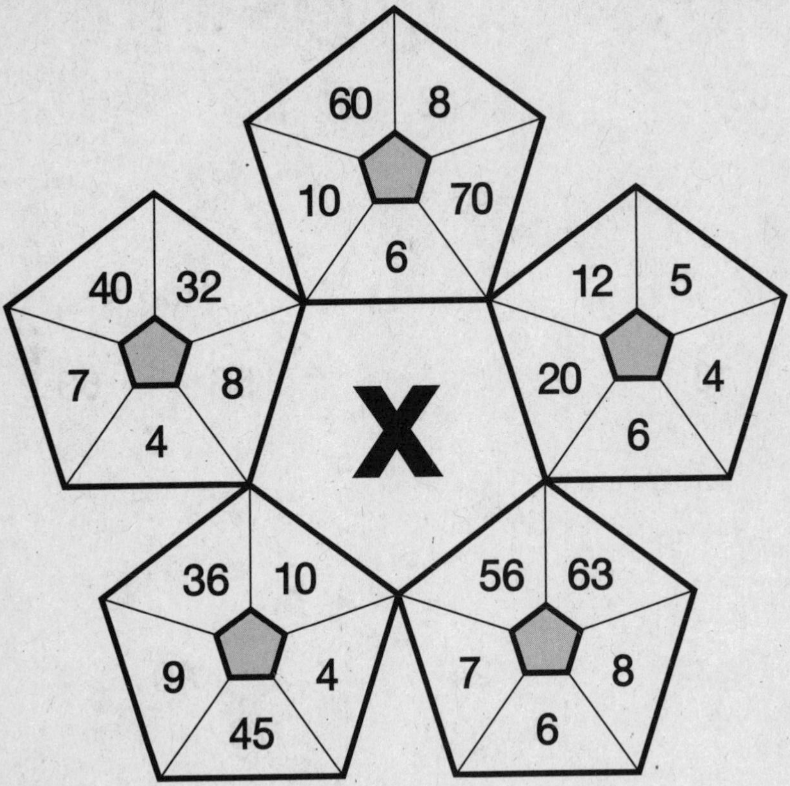

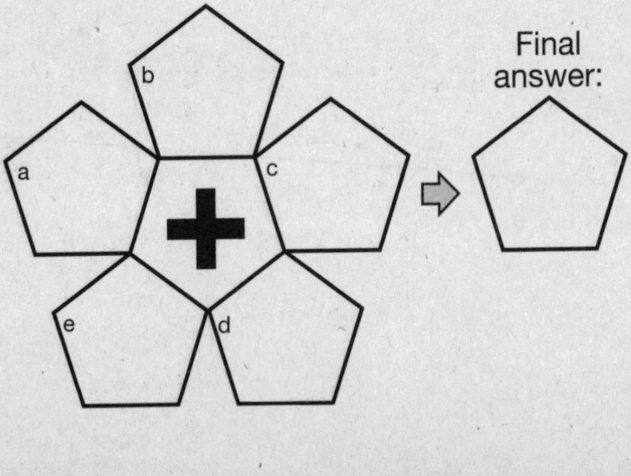

KAKOOMA EASY 5 MULTIPLICATION

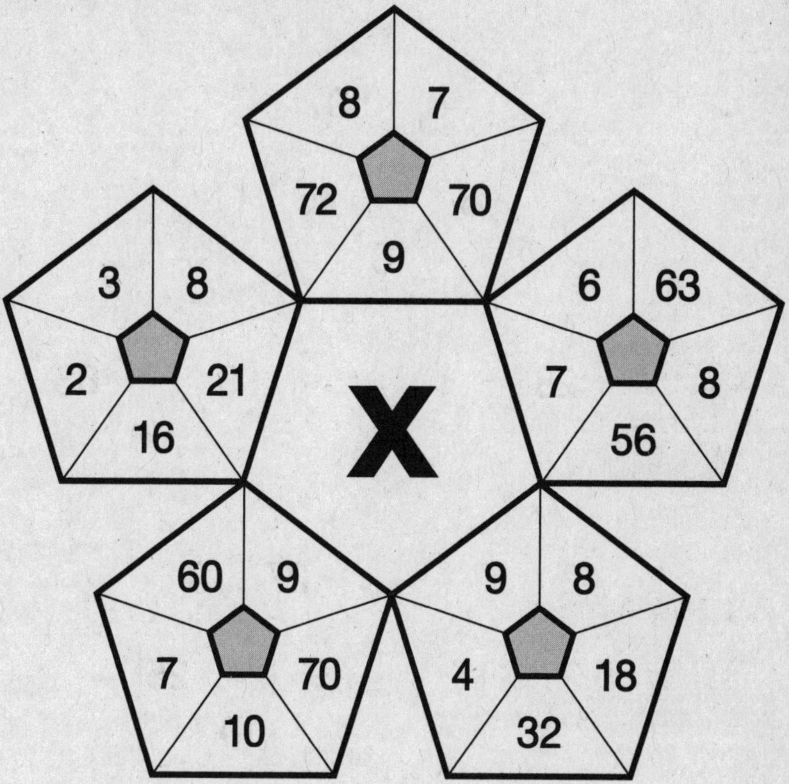

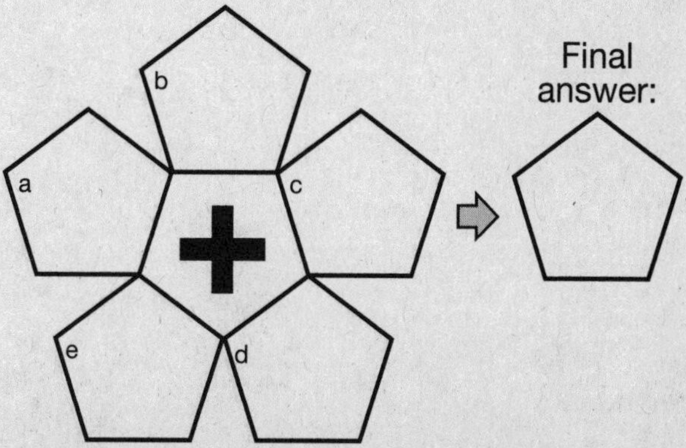

KAKOOMA EASY 5 MULTIPLICATION

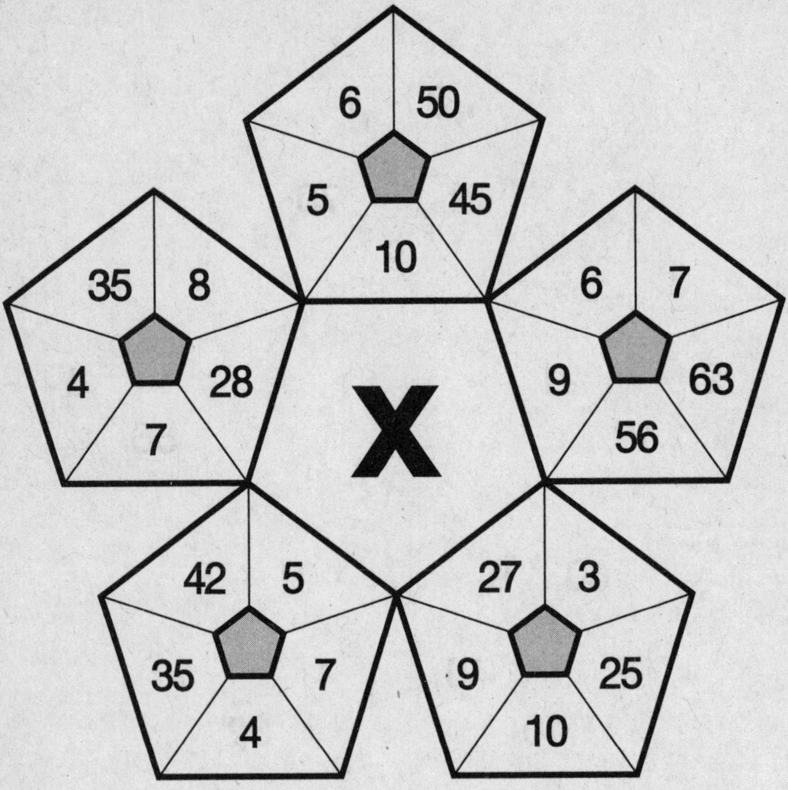

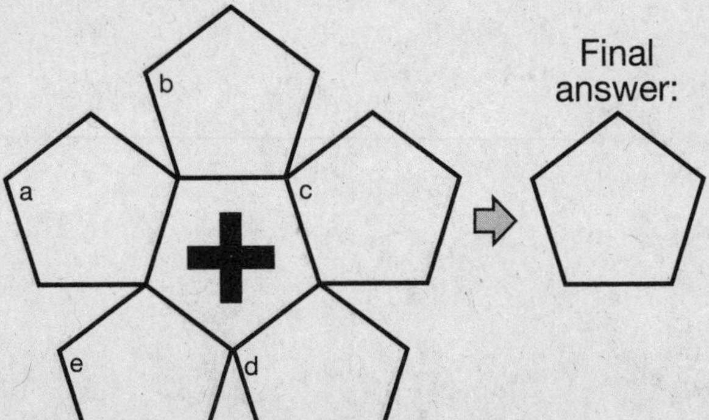

KAKOOMA EASY 6 MULTIPLICATION

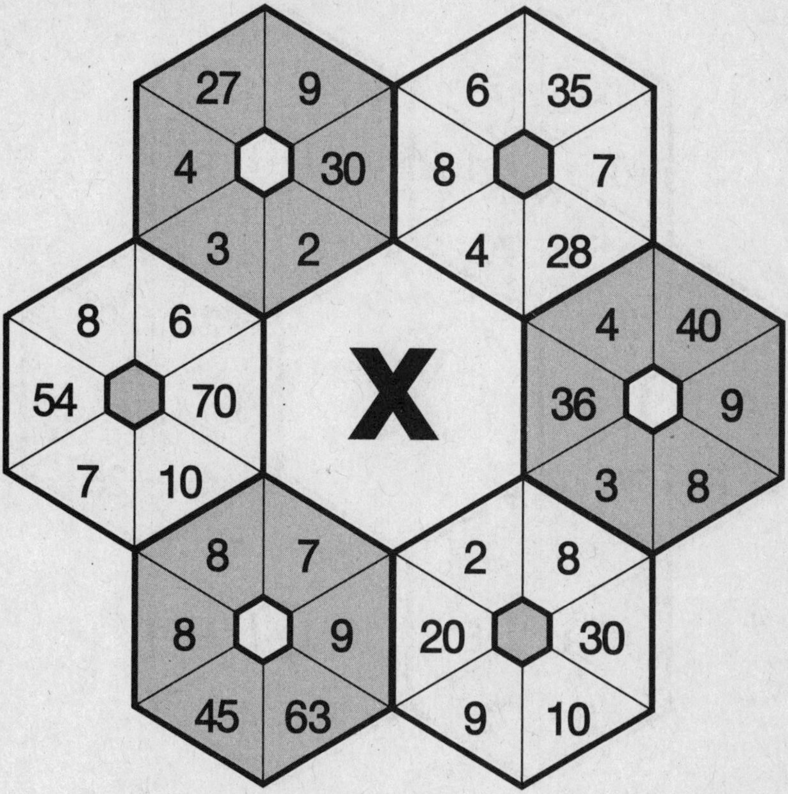

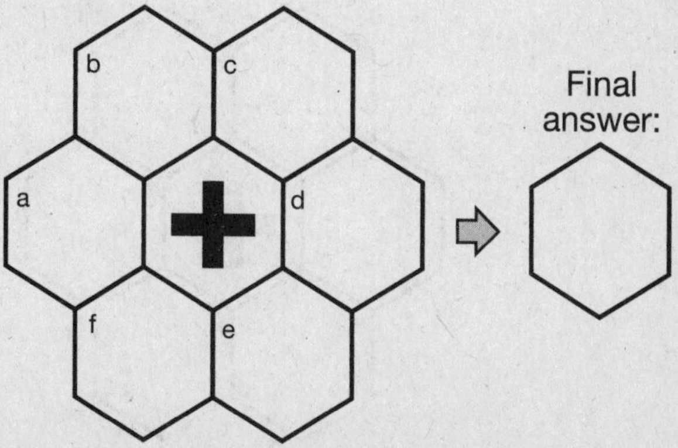

KAKOOMA EASY 6 MULTIPLICATION

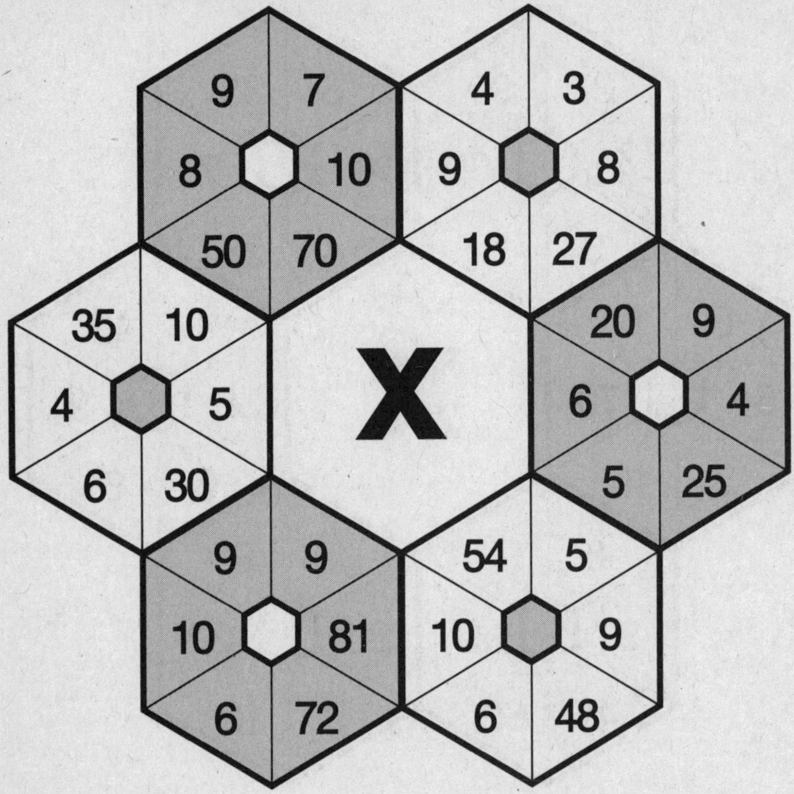

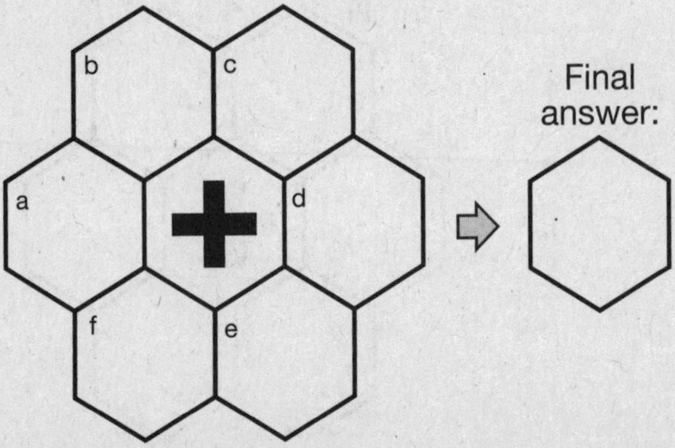

KAKOOMA EASY 6 MULTIPLICATION

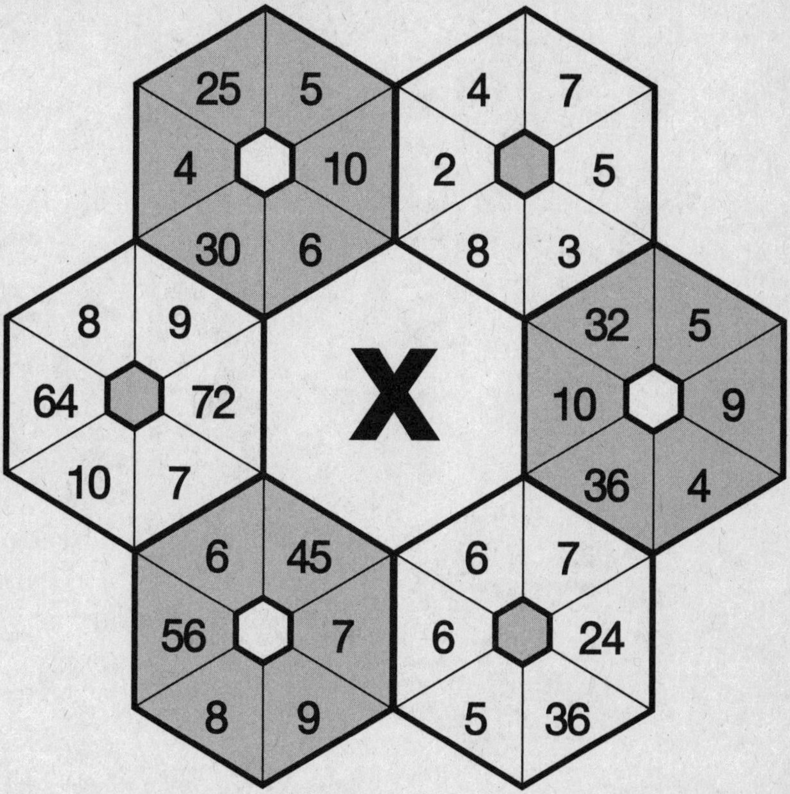

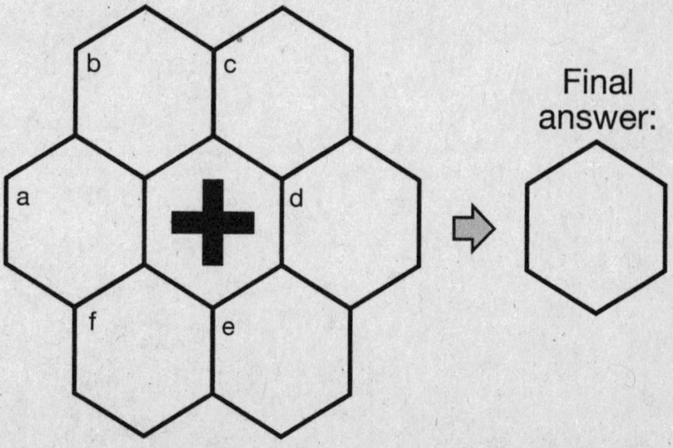

KAKOOMA EASY 6 MULTIPLICATION

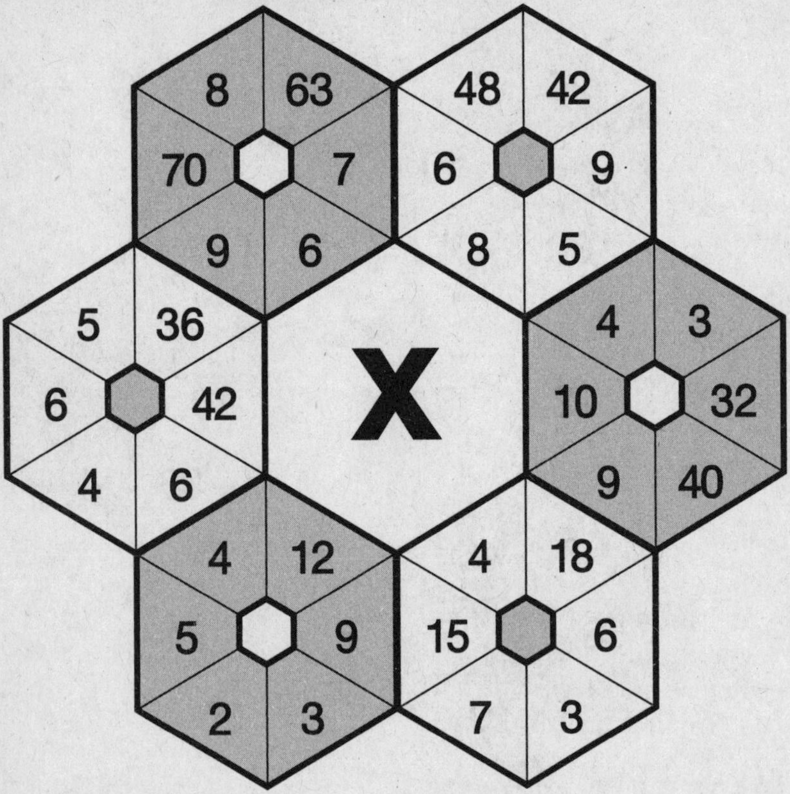

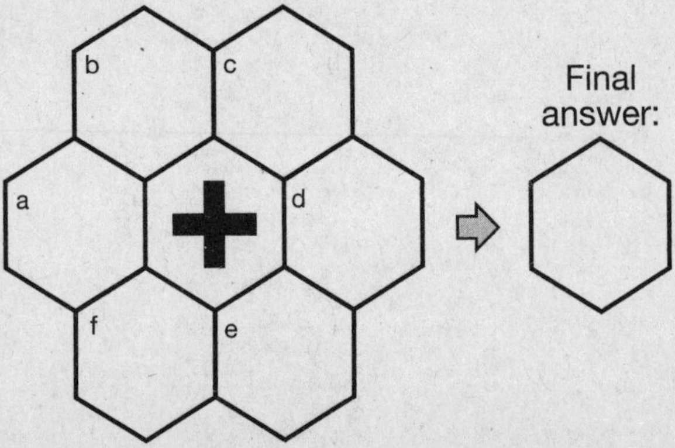

KAKOOMA EASY 6 MULTIPLICATION

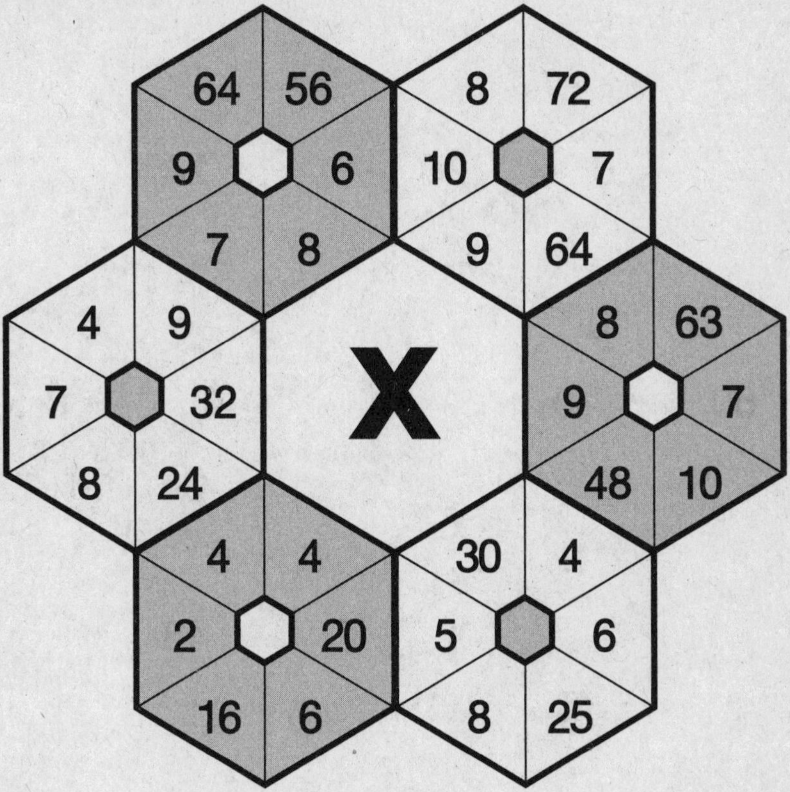

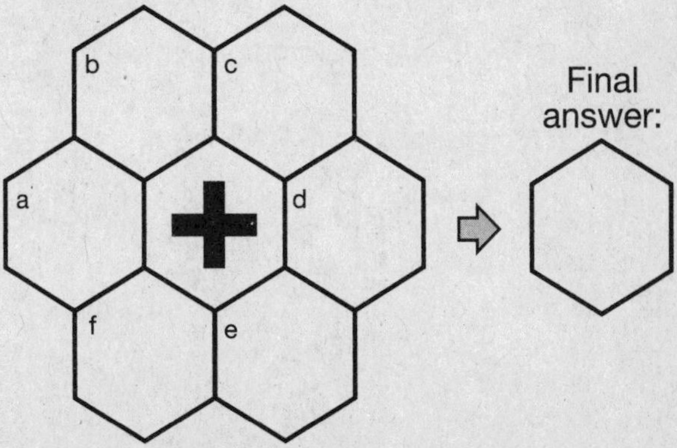

KAKOOMA EASY 6 MULTIPLICATION

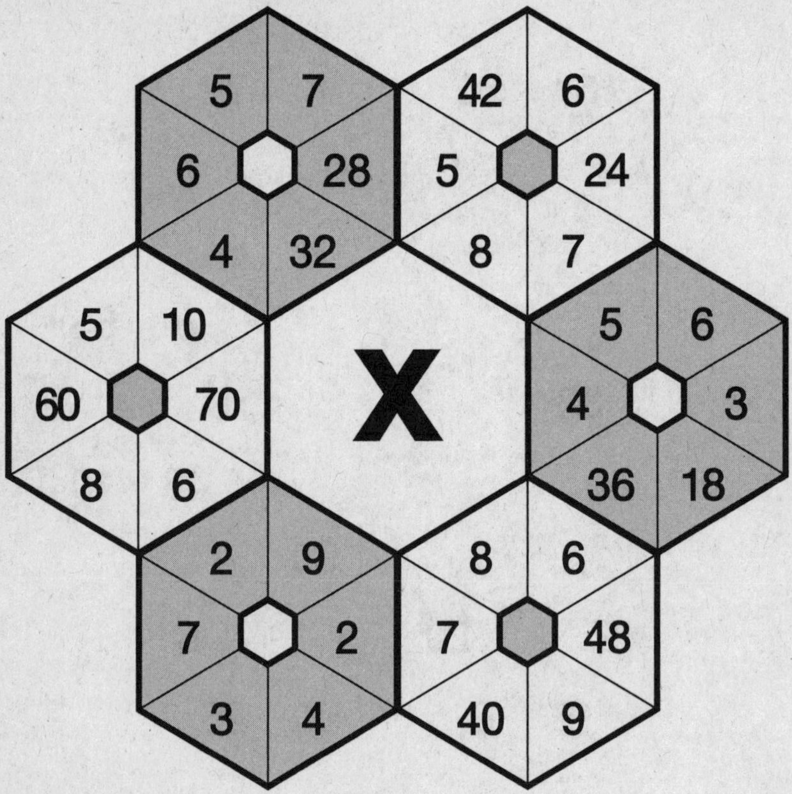

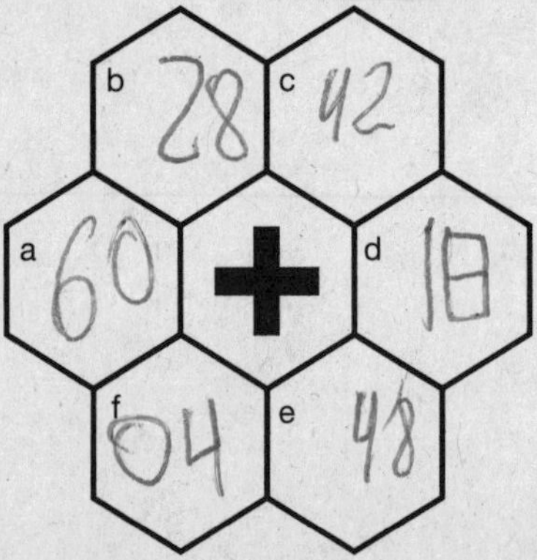

Final answer:

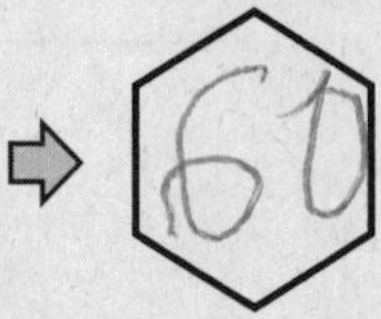

KAKOOMA EASY 6 MULTIPLICATION

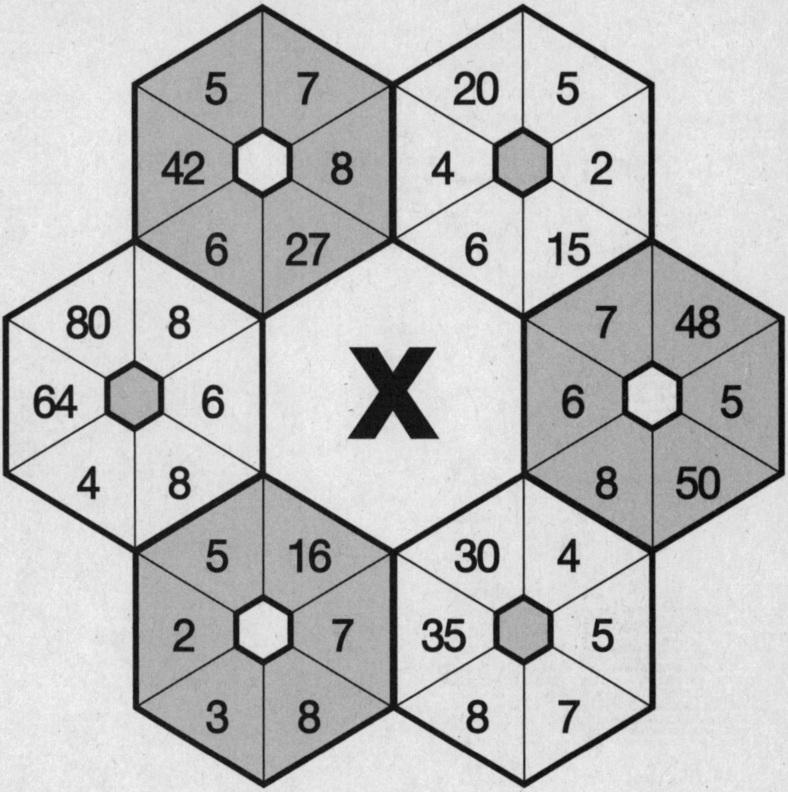

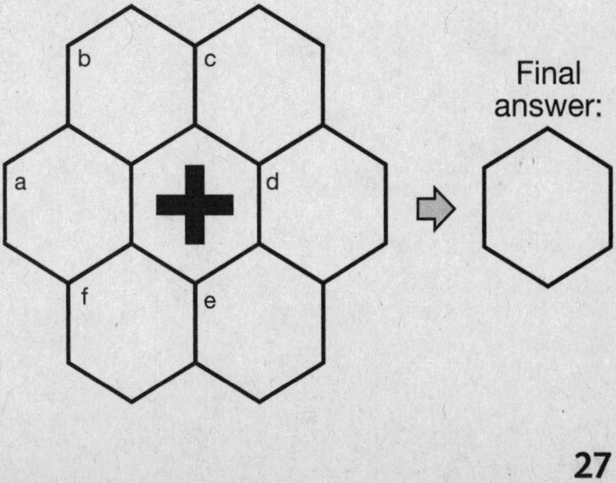

KAKOOMA EASY 6 MULTIPLICATION

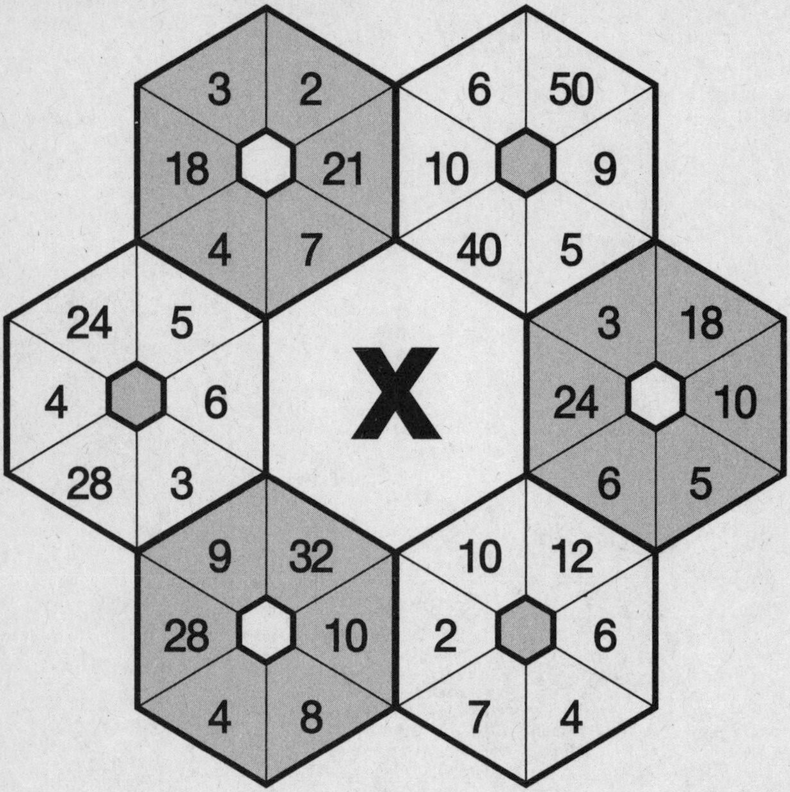

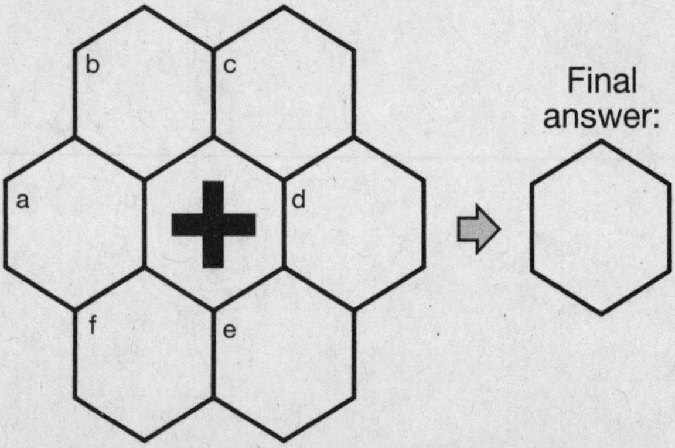

KAKOOMA EASY 6 MULTIPLICATION

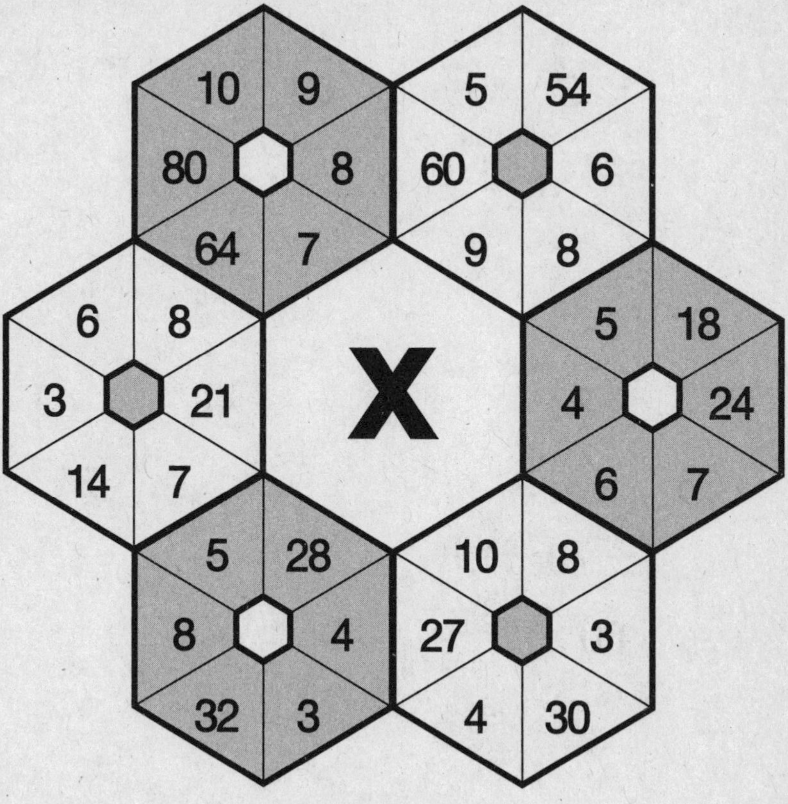

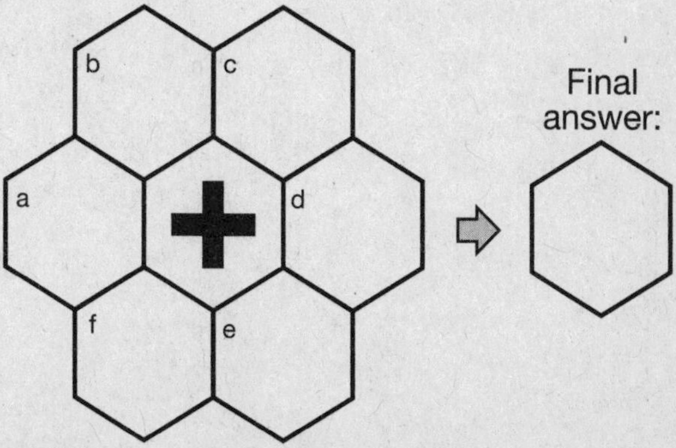

KAKOOMA EASY 6 MULTIPLICATION

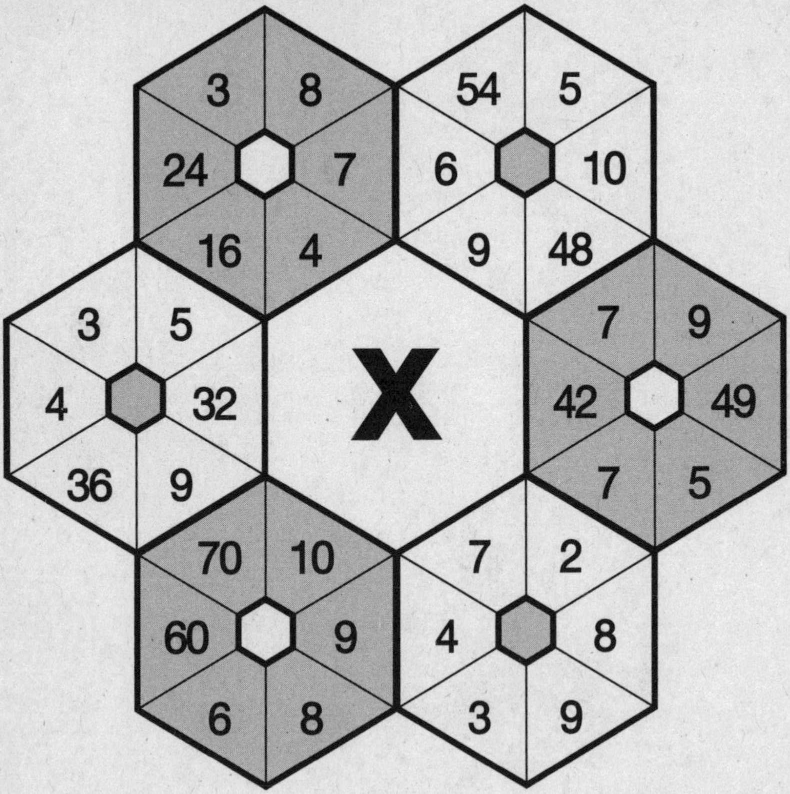

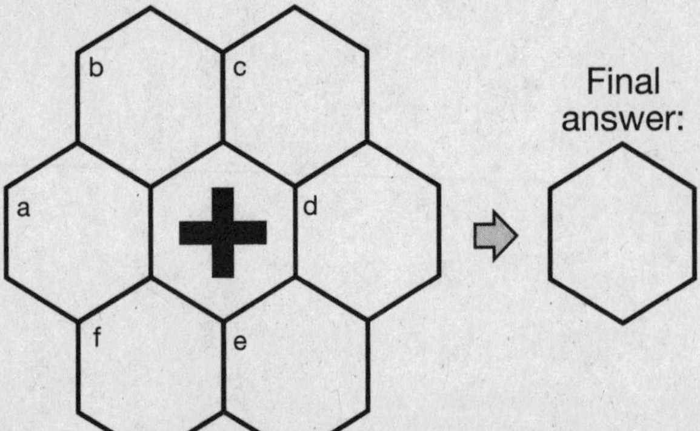

KAKOOMA EASY 6 MULTIPLICATION

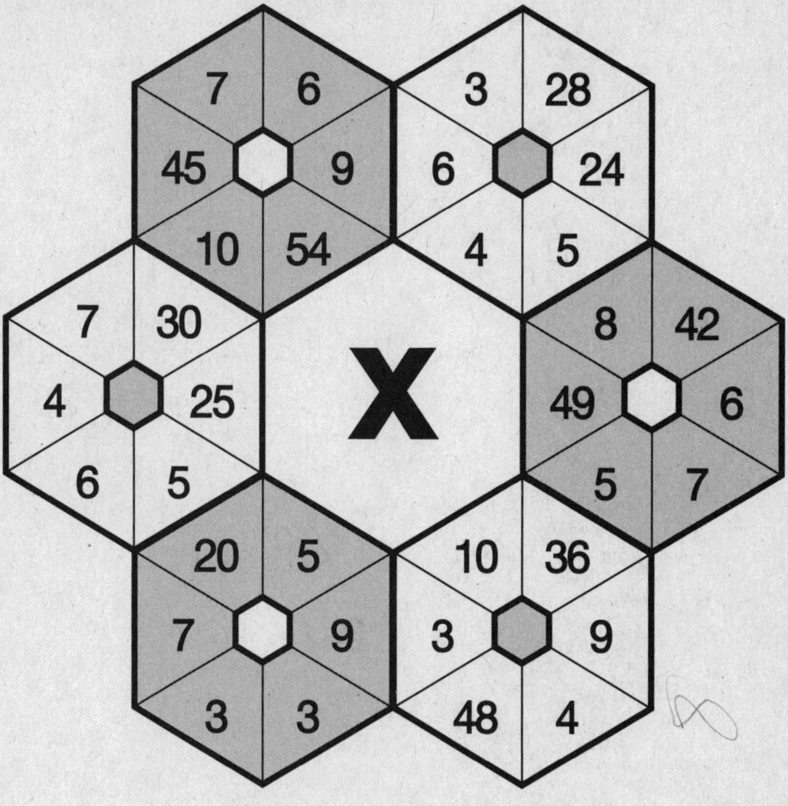

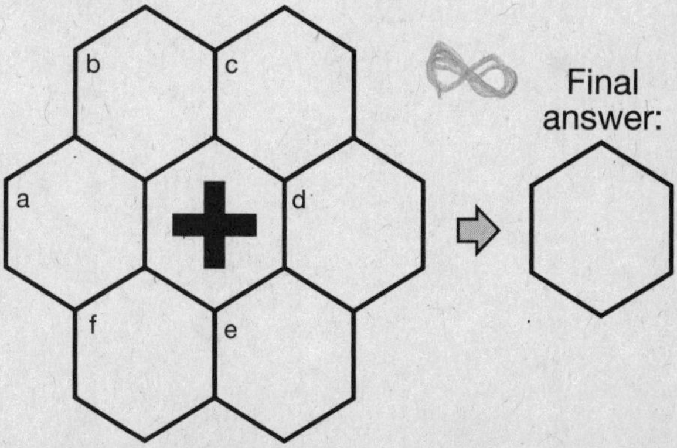

KAKOOMA EASY 6 MULTIPLICATION

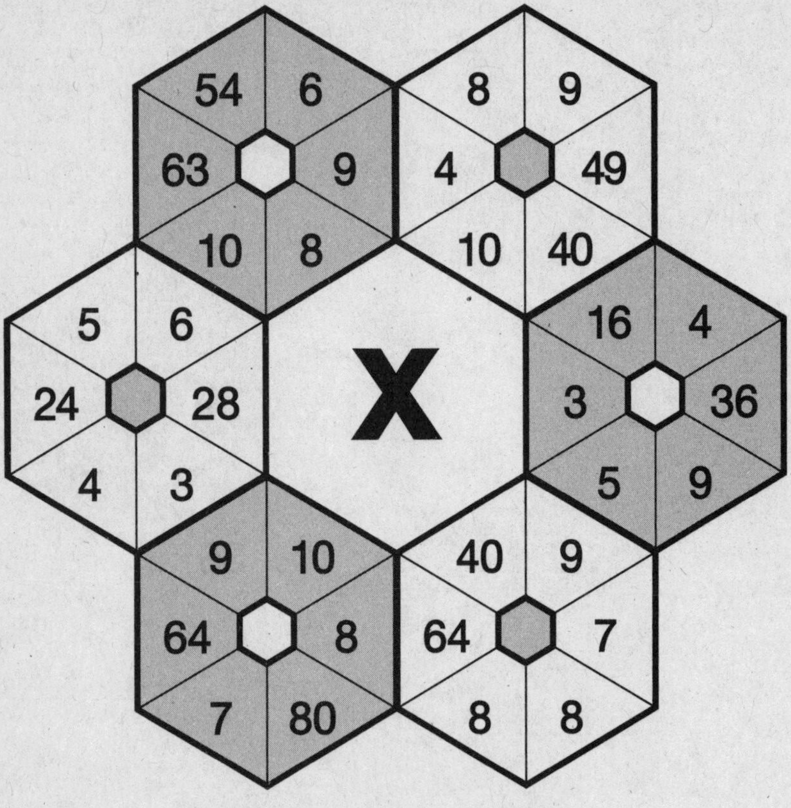

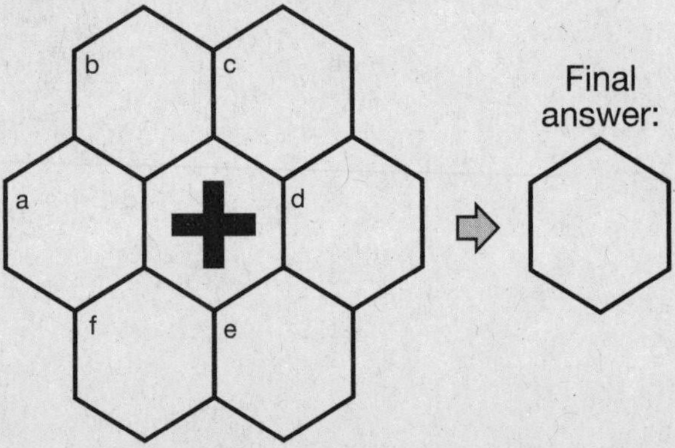

KAKOOMA EASY 6 MULTIPLICATION

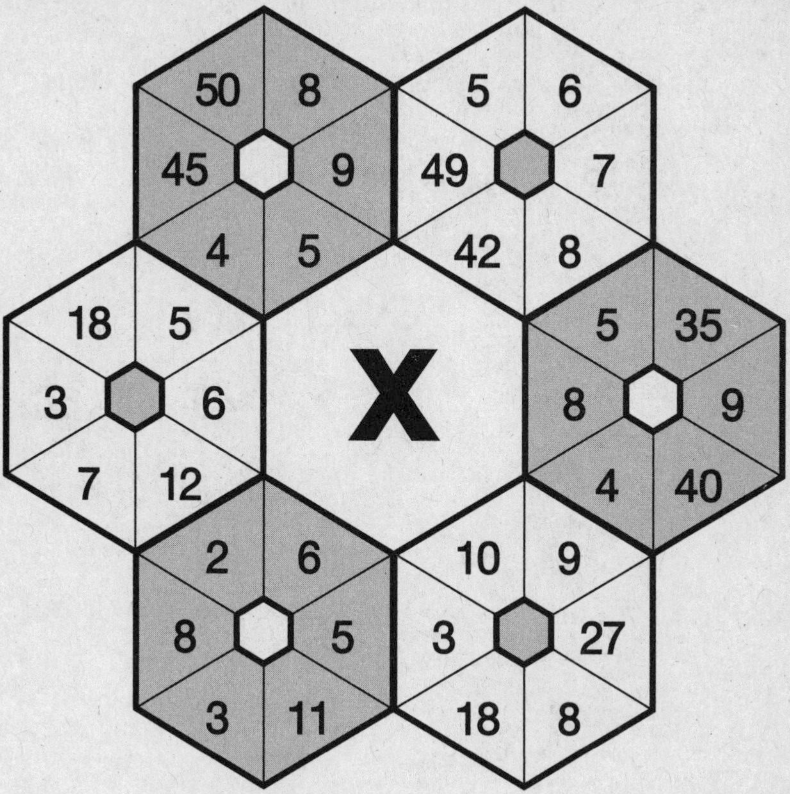

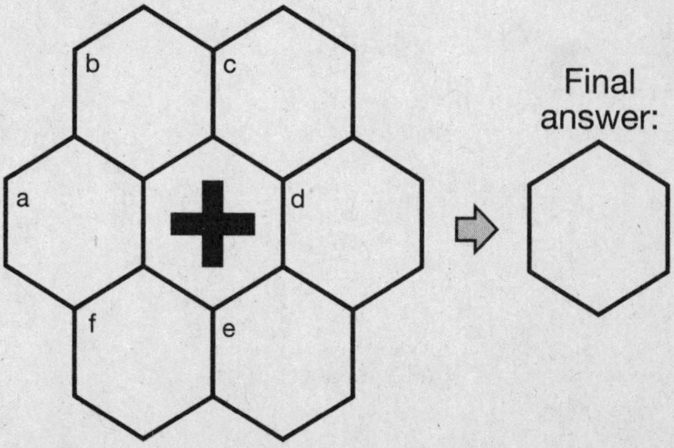

KAKOOMA EASY 6 MULTIPLICATION

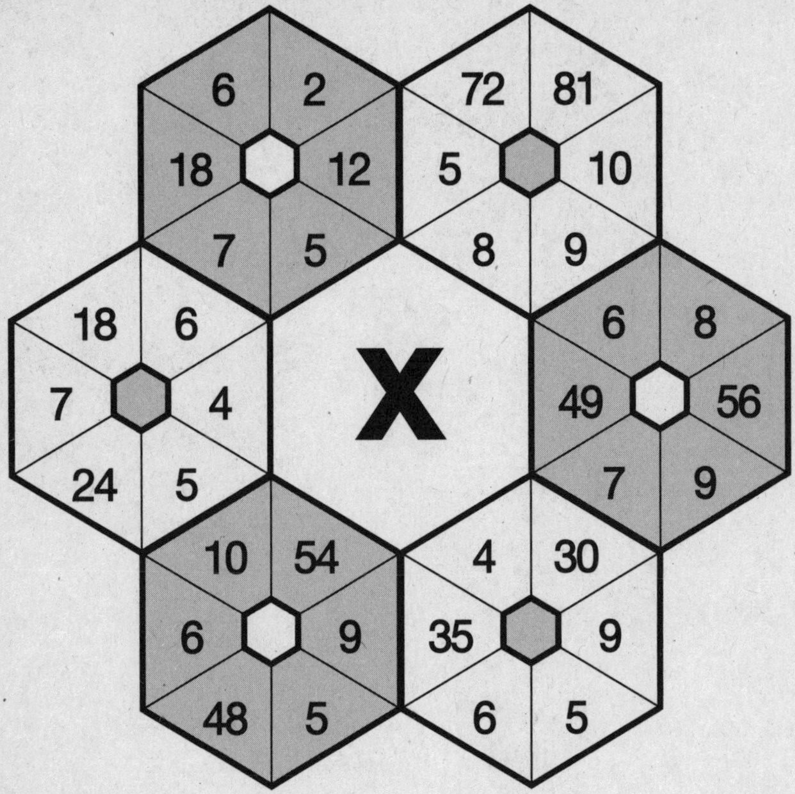

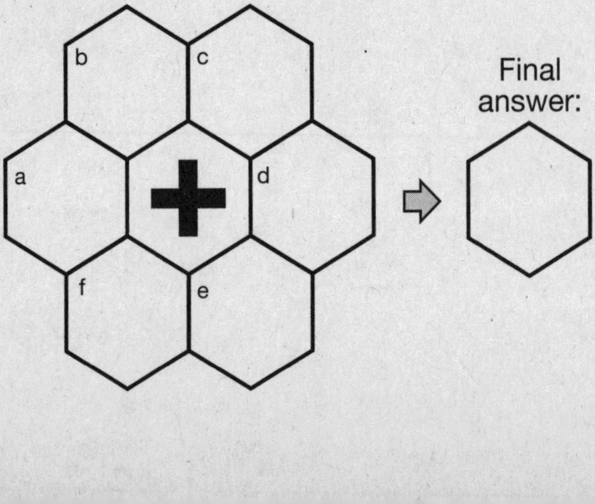

KAKOOMA EASY 6 MULTIPLICATION

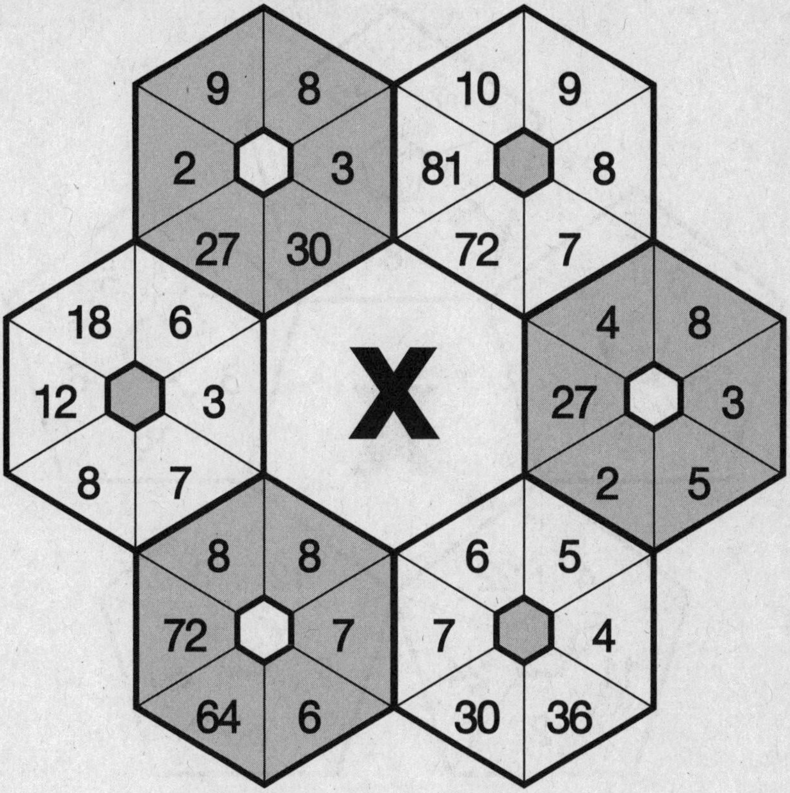

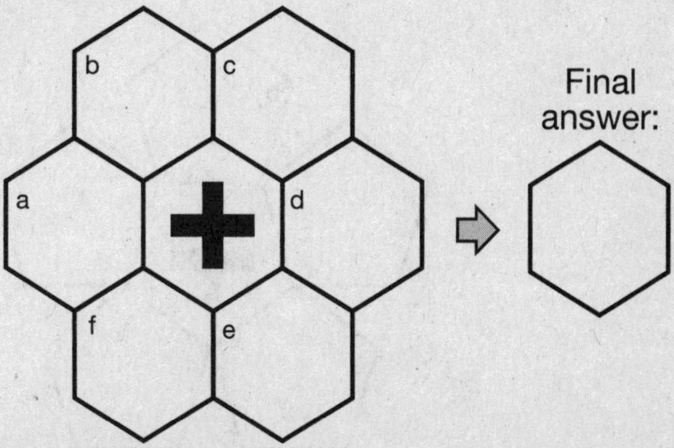

KAKOOMA HARD 5 MULTIPLICATION

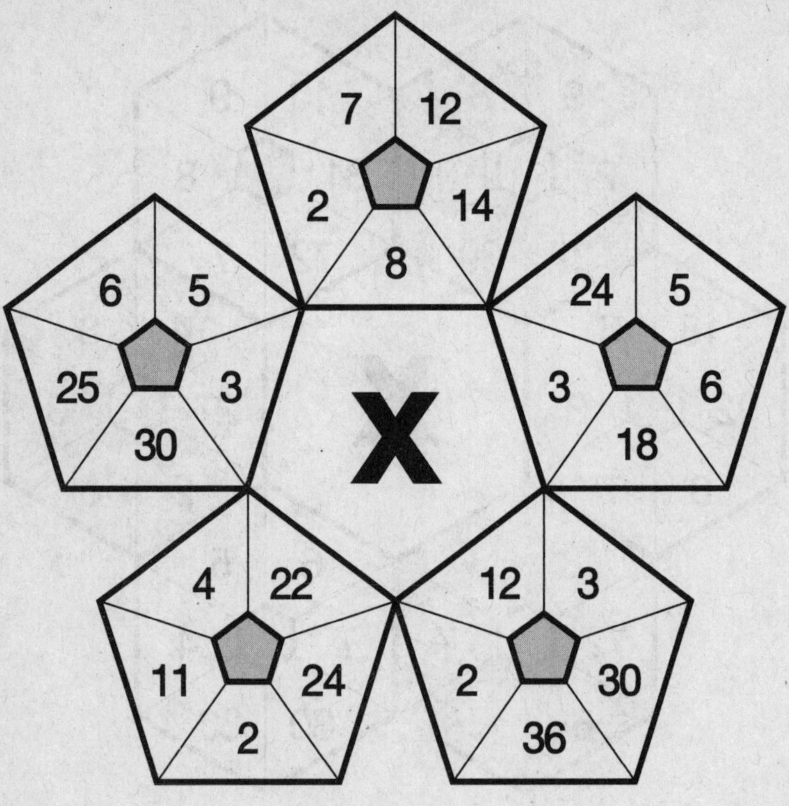

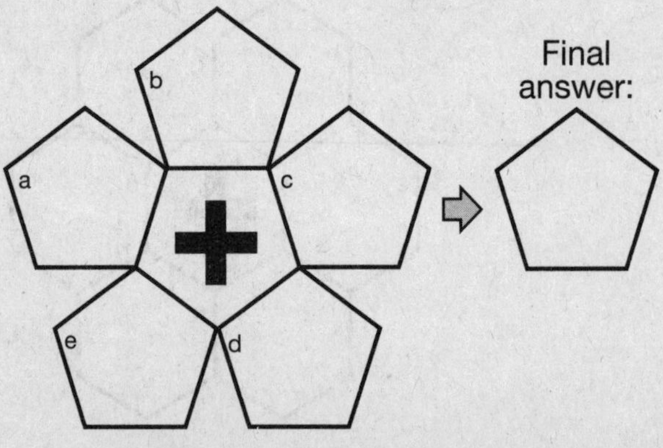

KAKOOMA HARD 5 MULTIPLICATION

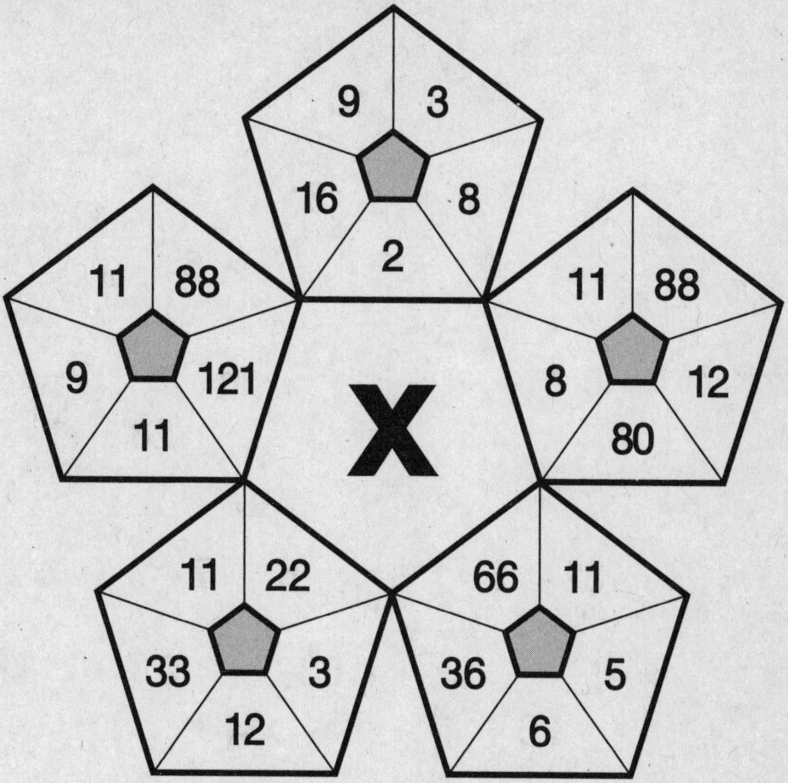

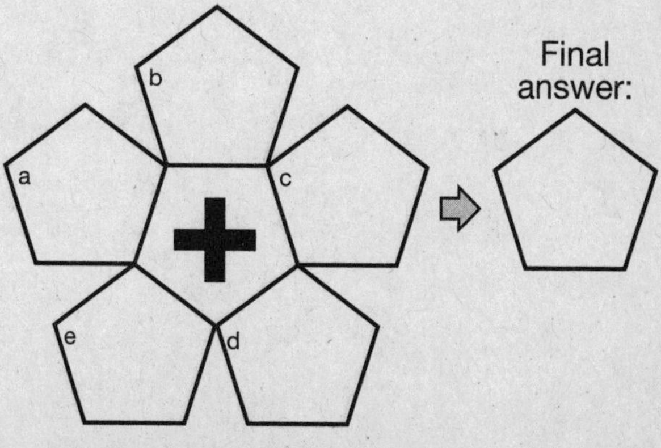

KAKOOMA HARD 5 MULTIPLICATION

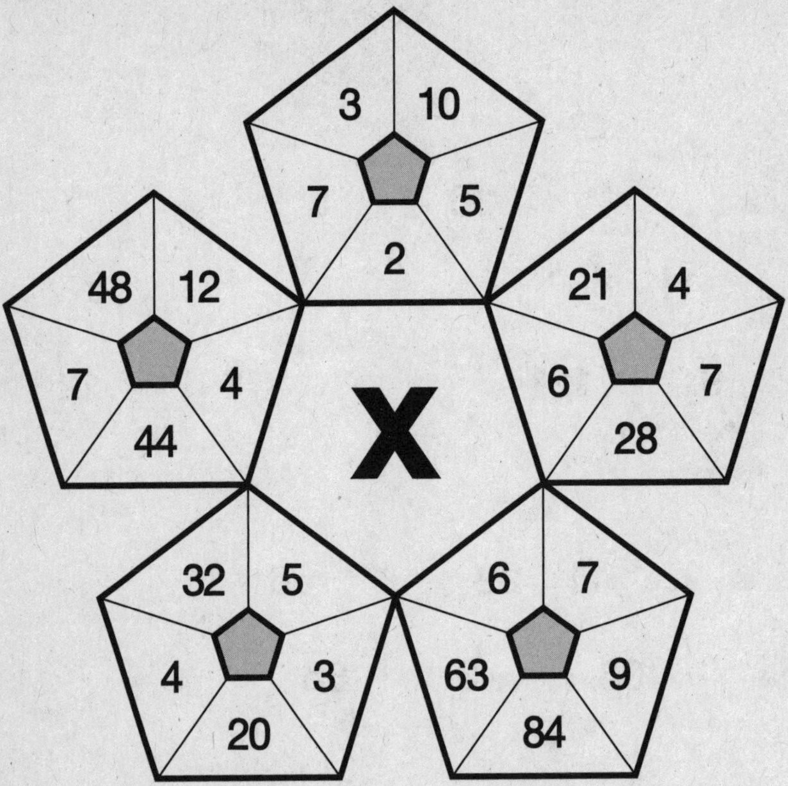

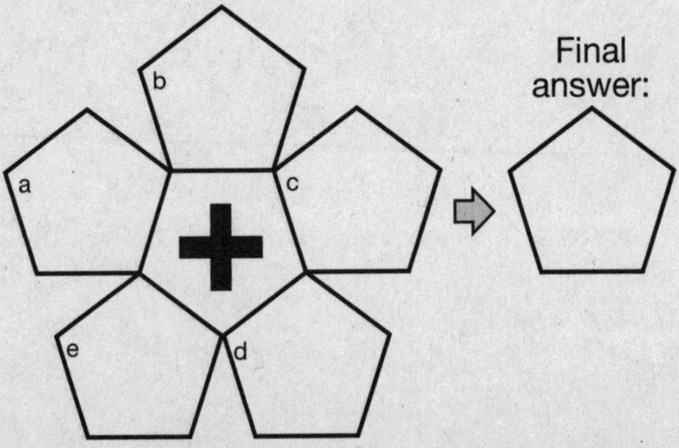

KAKOOMA HARD 5 MULTIPLICATION

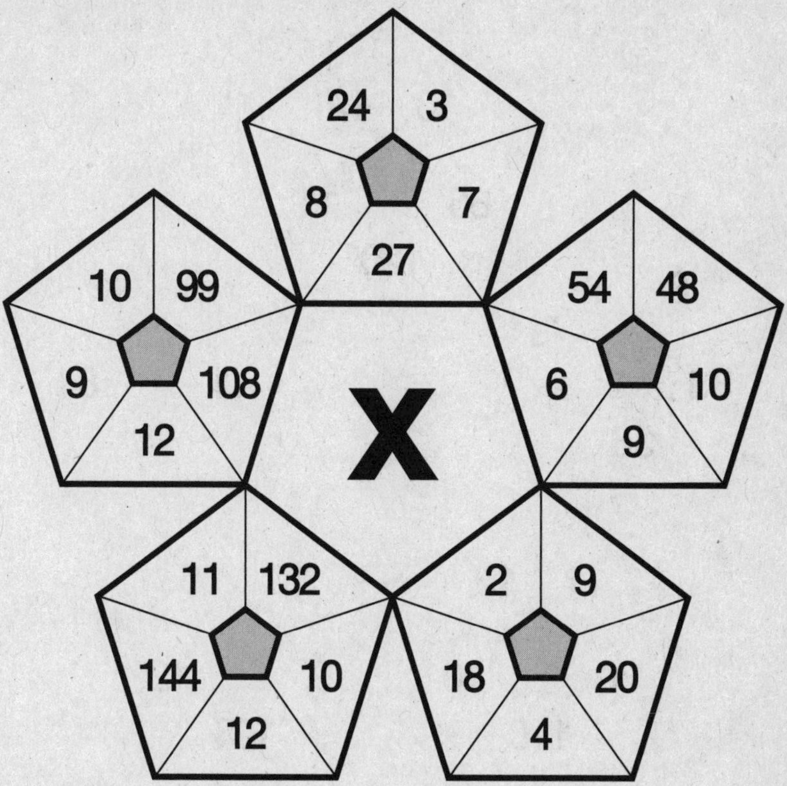

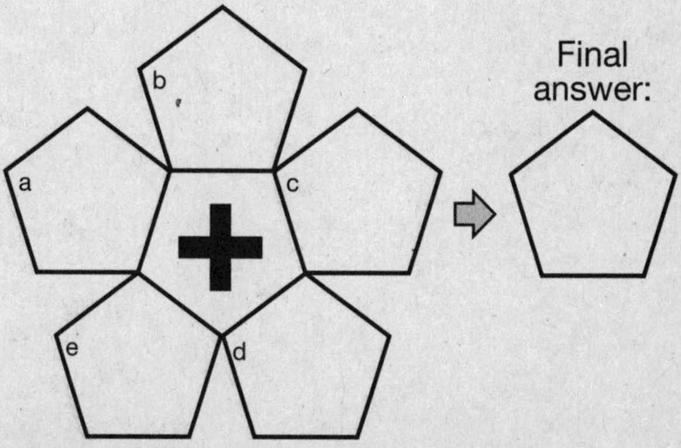

KAKOOMA HARD 5 MULTIPLICATION

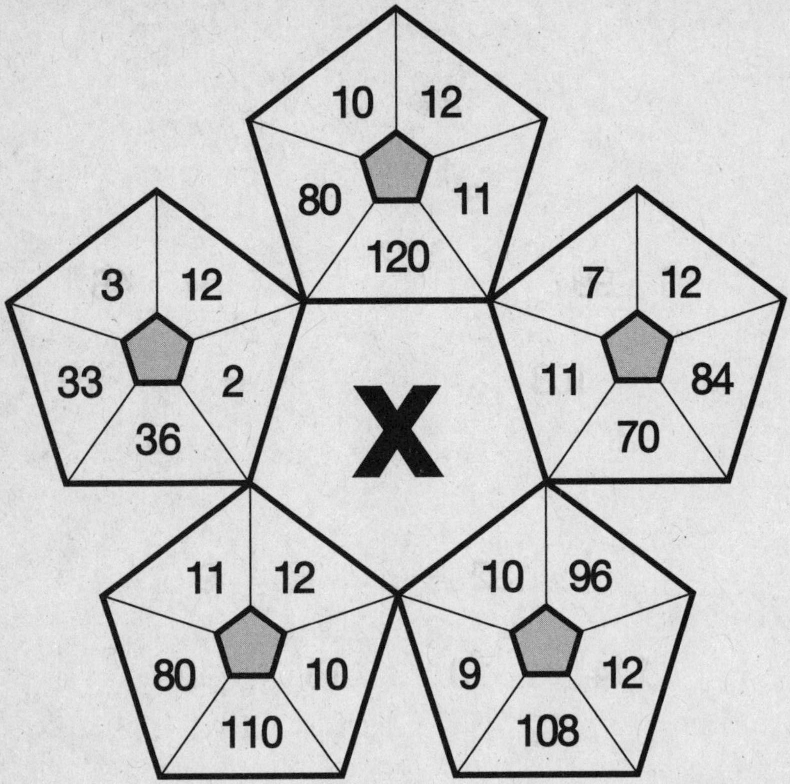

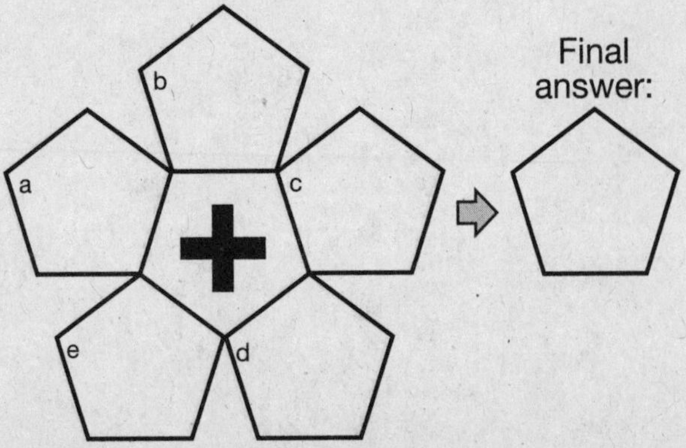

KAKOOMA HARD 5 MULTIPLICATION

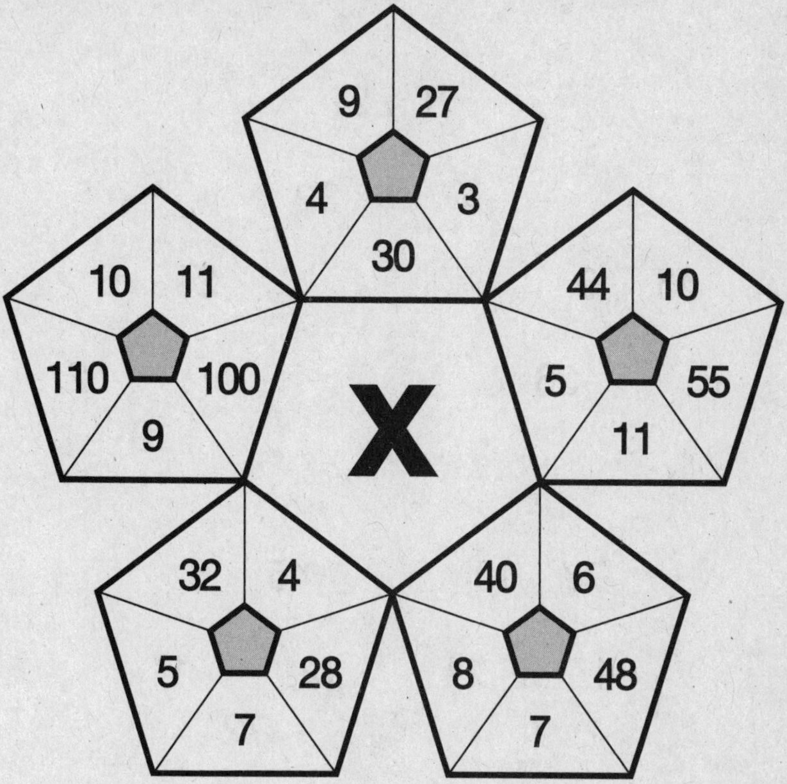

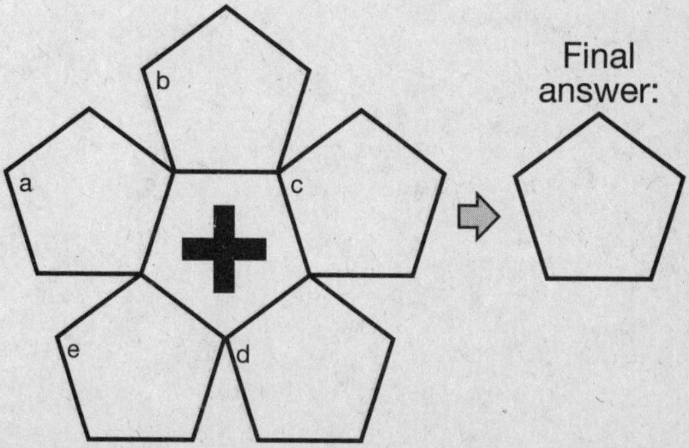

KAKOOMA HARD 5 MULTIPLICATION

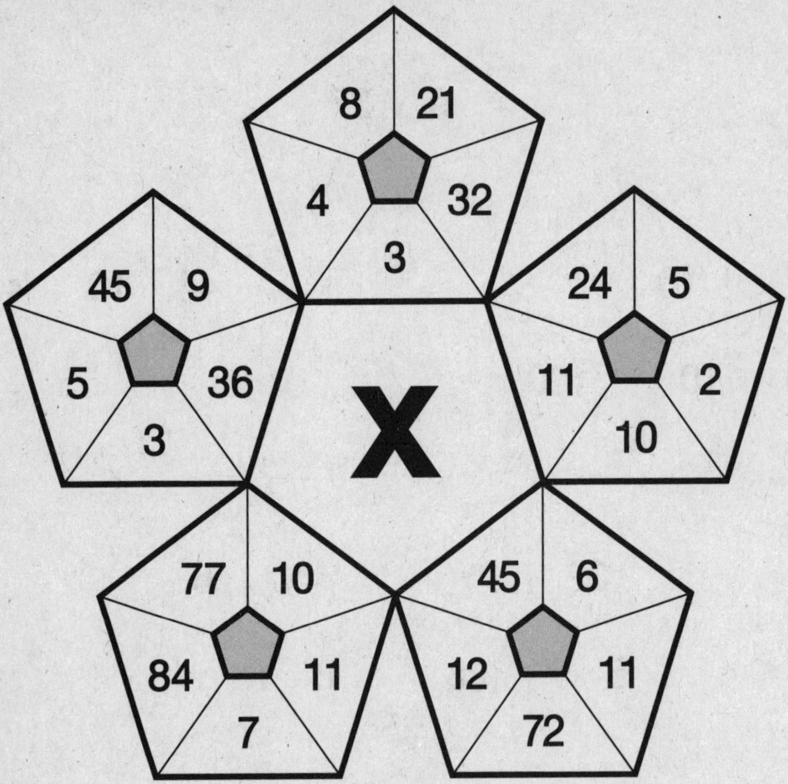

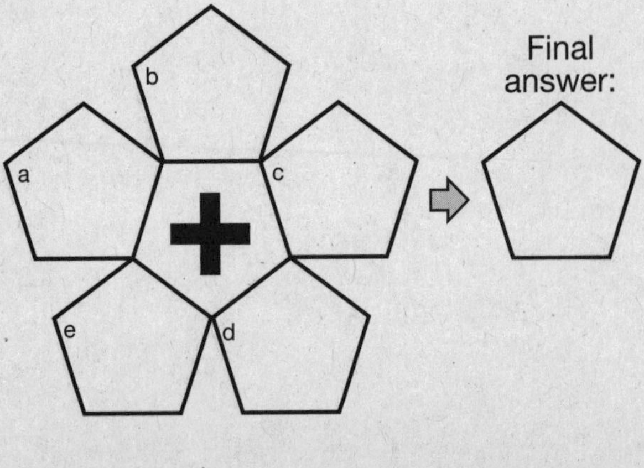

KAKOOMA HARD 5 MULTIPLICATION

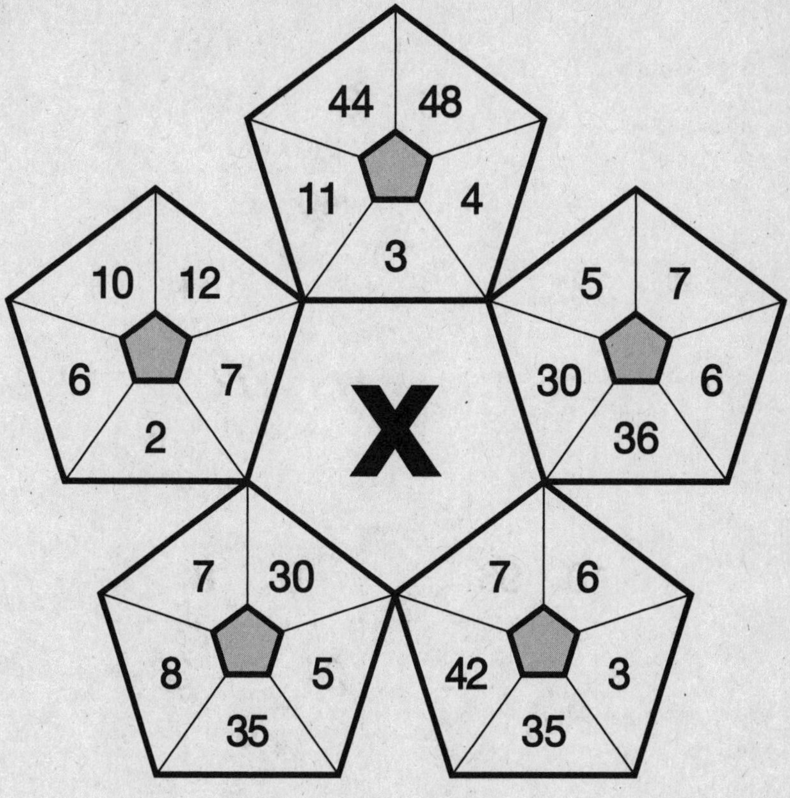

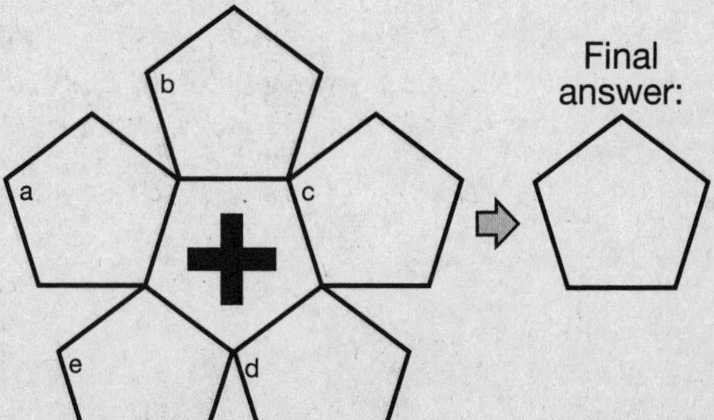

KAKOOMA HARD 5 MULTIPLICATION

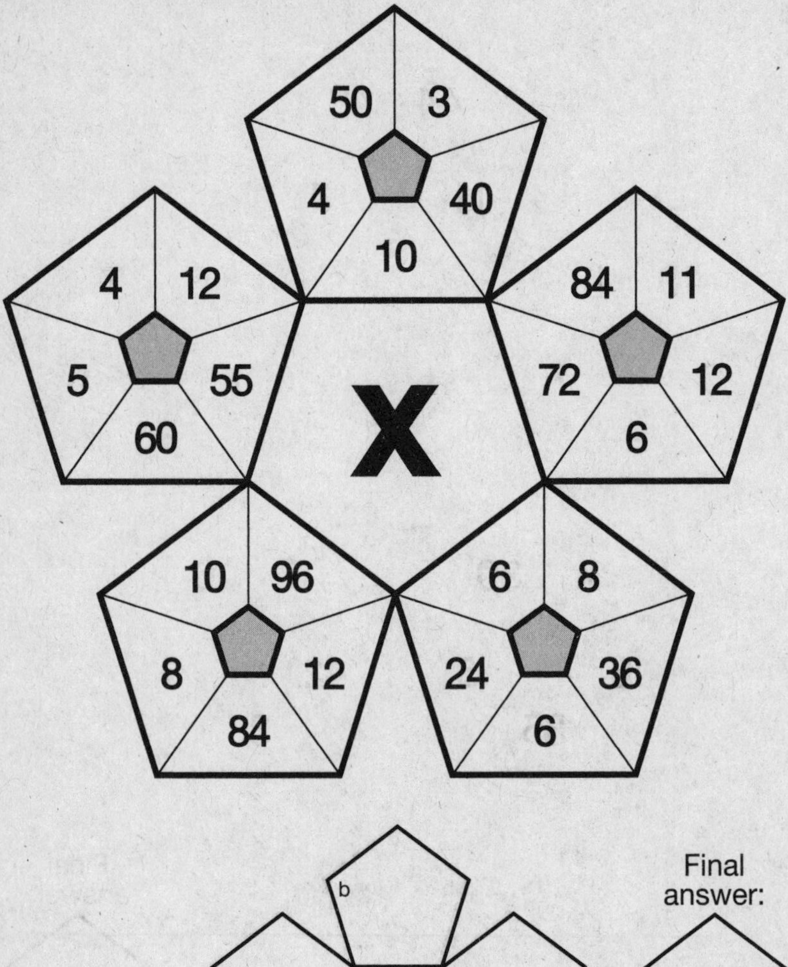

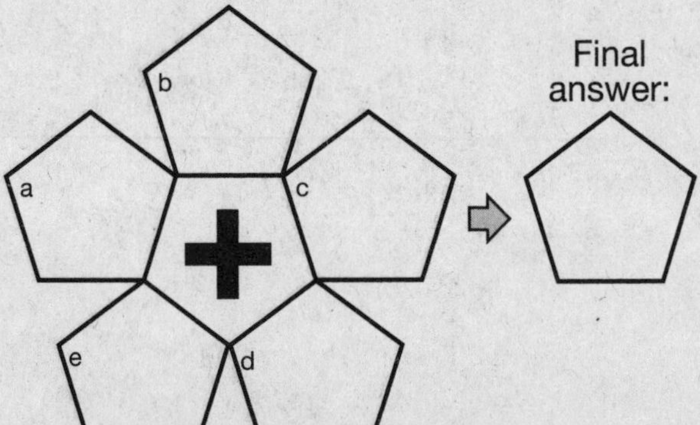

KAKOOMA HARD 5 MULTIPLICATION

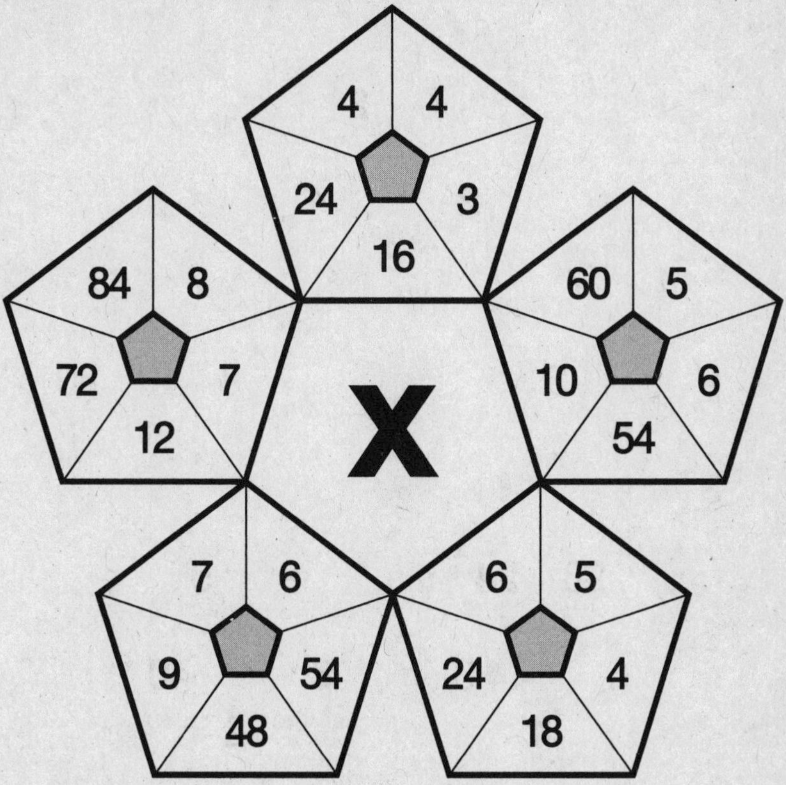

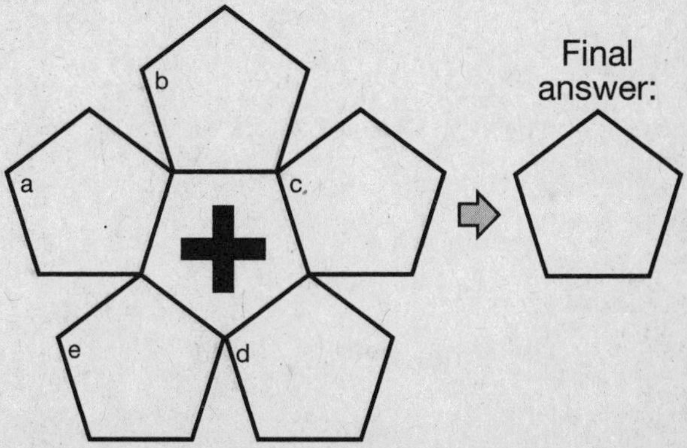

KAKOOMA HARD 5 MULTIPLICATION

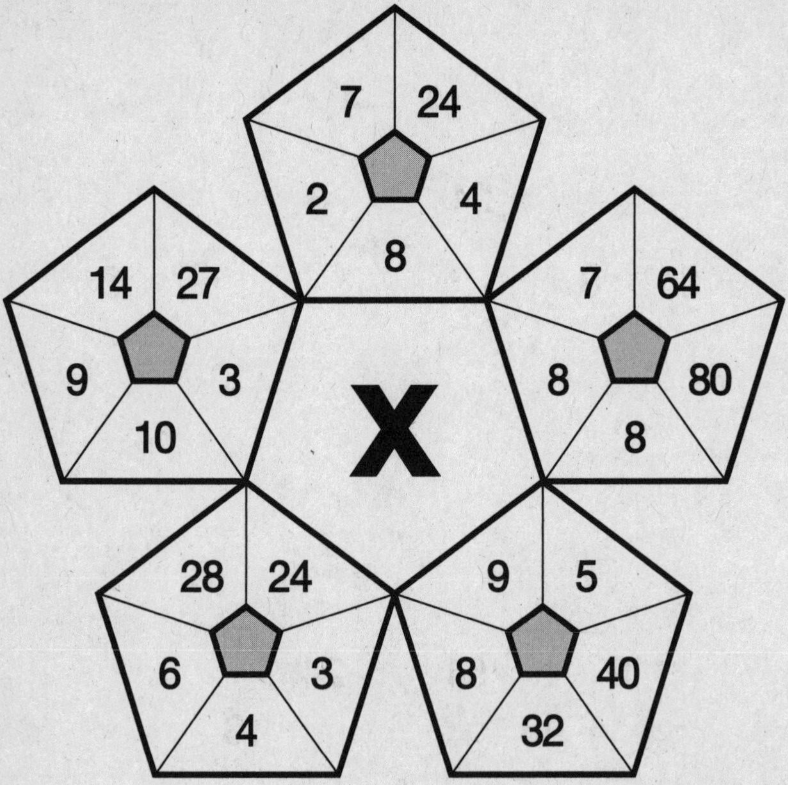

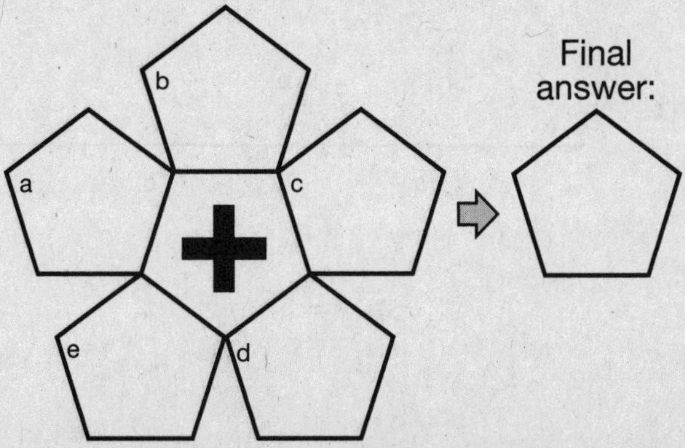

KAKOOMA HARD 5 MULTIPLICATION

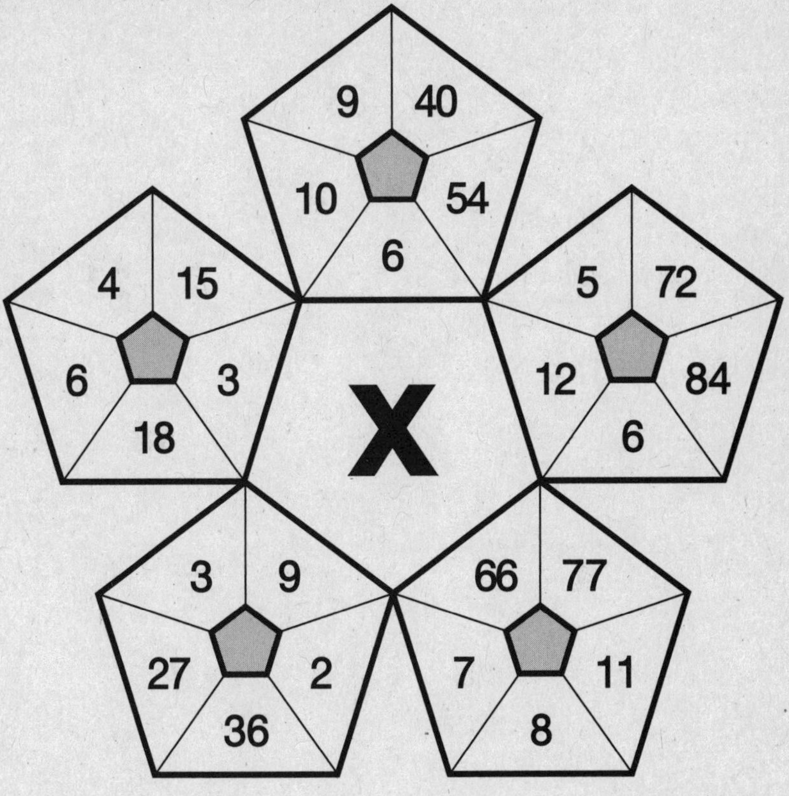

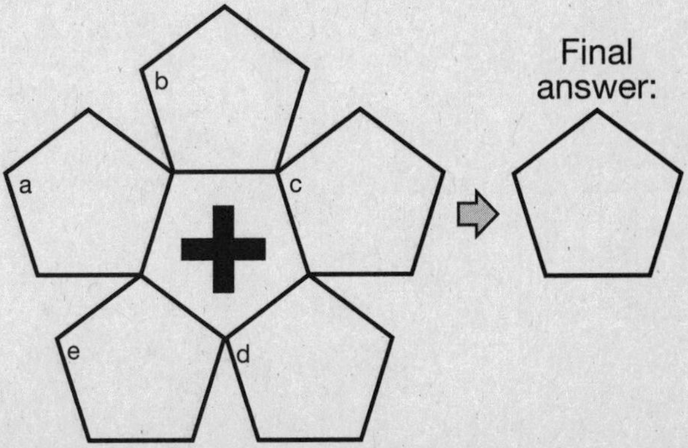

KAKOOMA HARD 5 MULTIPLICATION

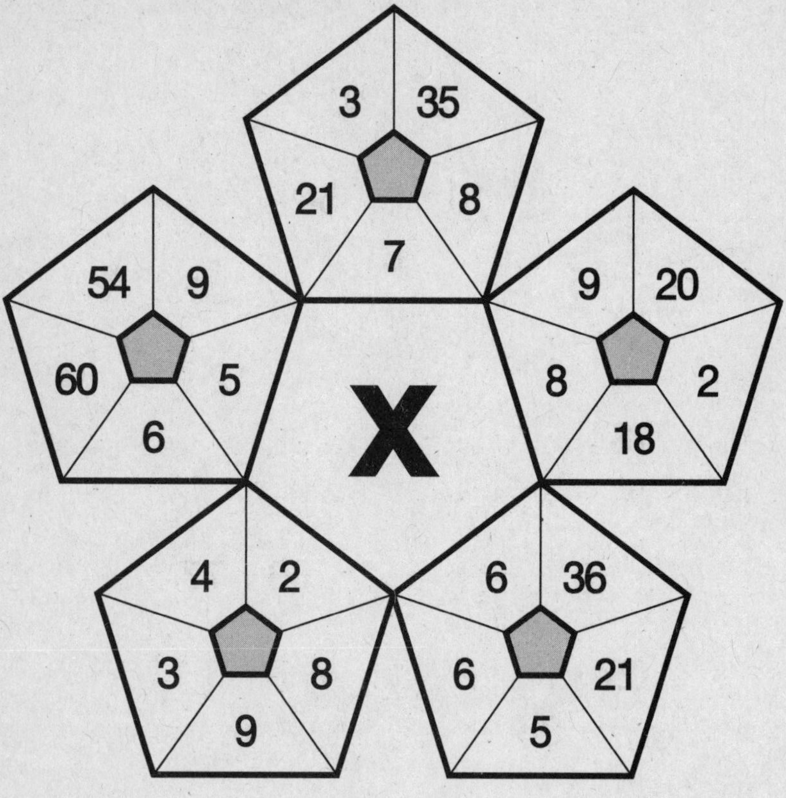

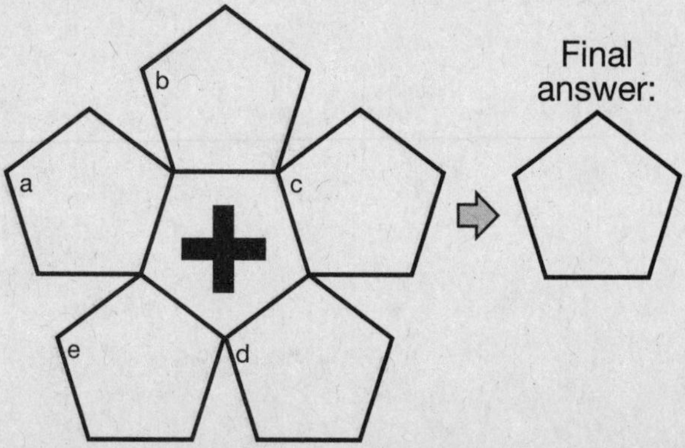

KAKOOMA HARD 5 MULTIPLICATION

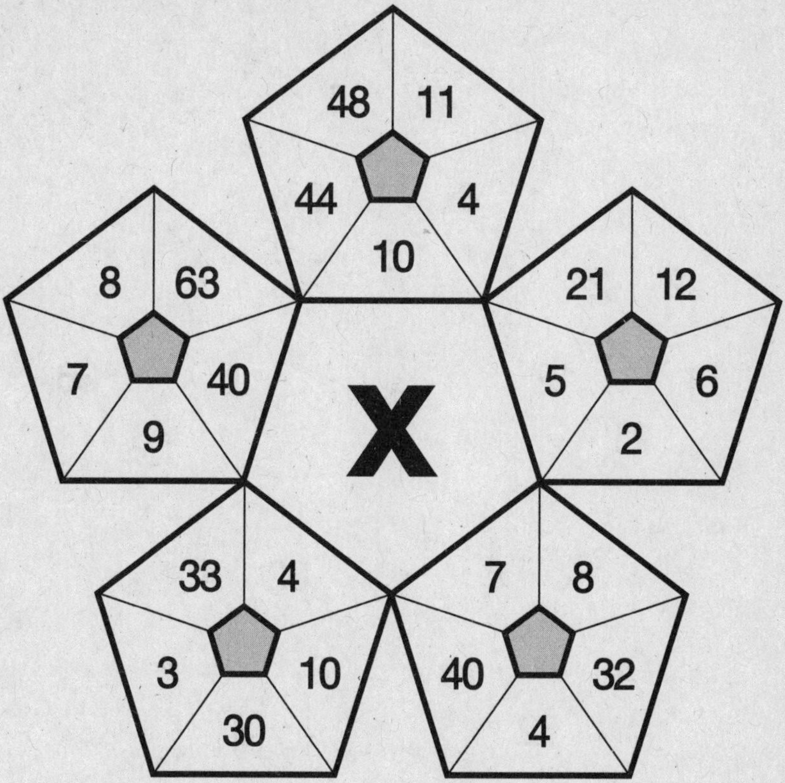

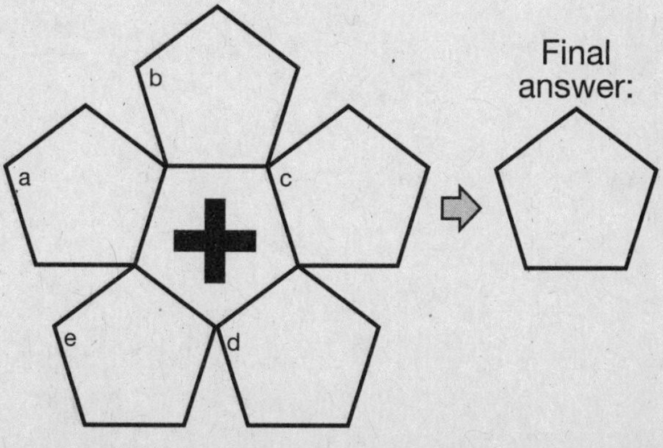

KAKOOMA HARD 5 MULTIPLICATION

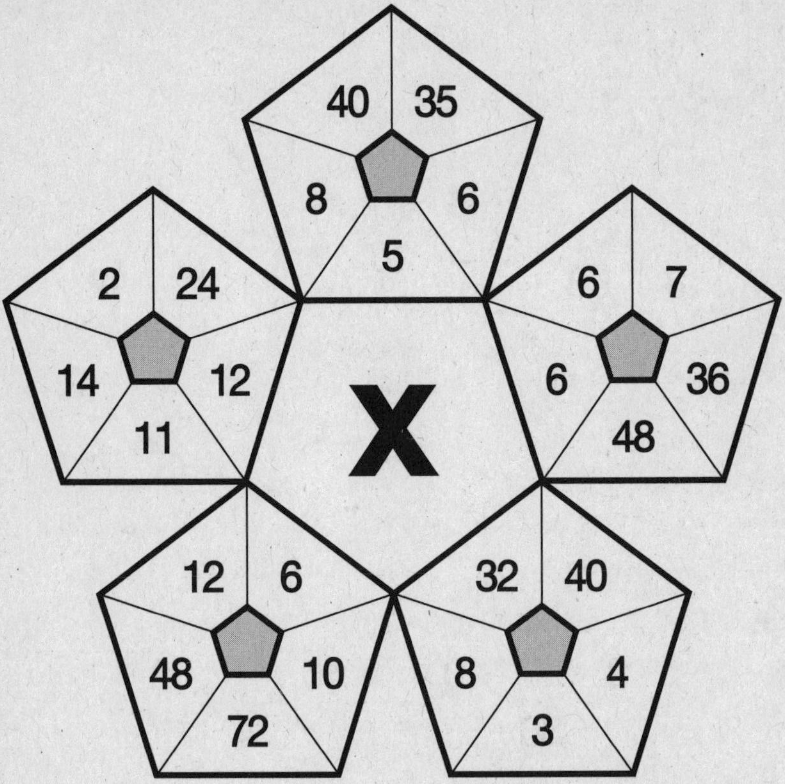

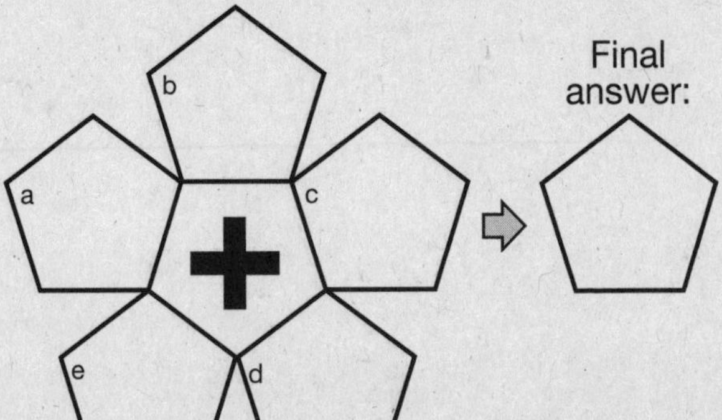

KAKOOMA HARD 5 MULTIPLICATION

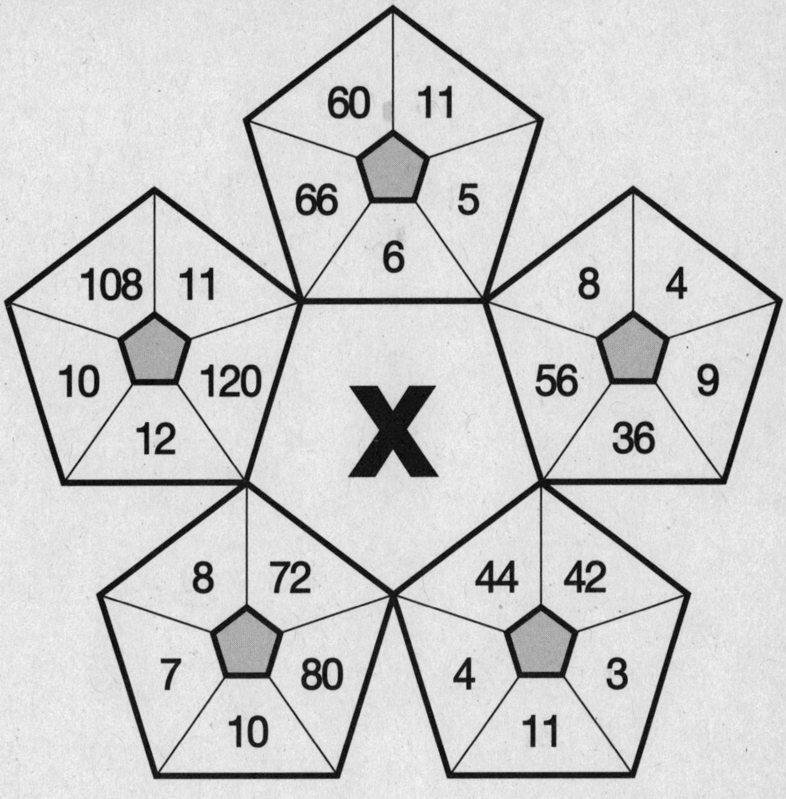

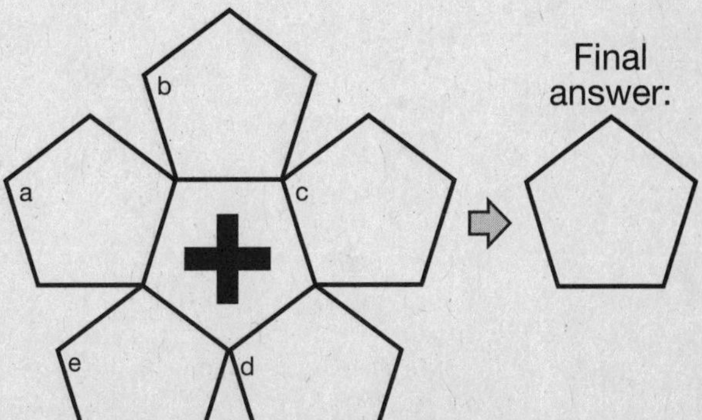

KAKOOMA HARD 5 MULTIPLICATION

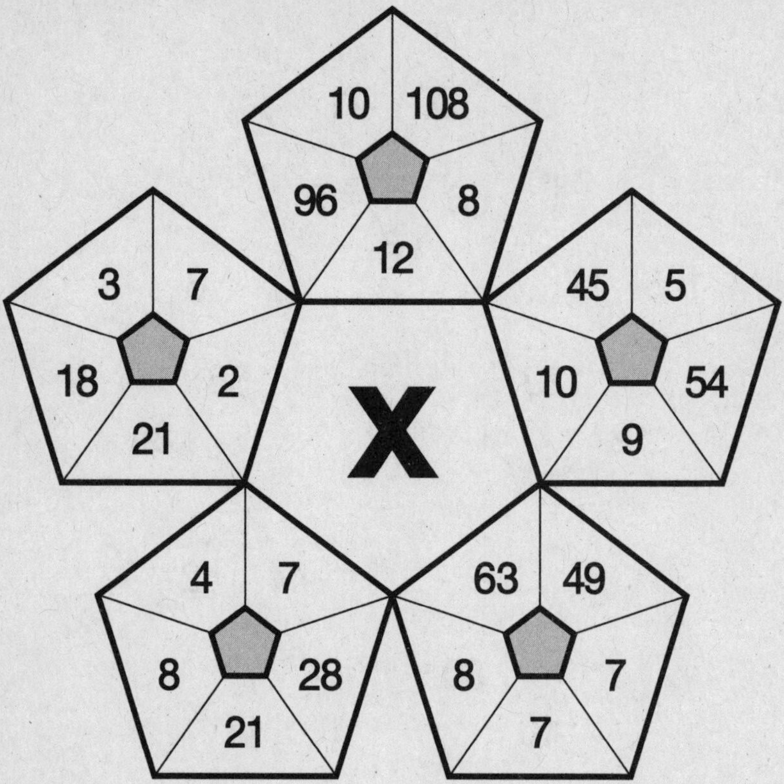

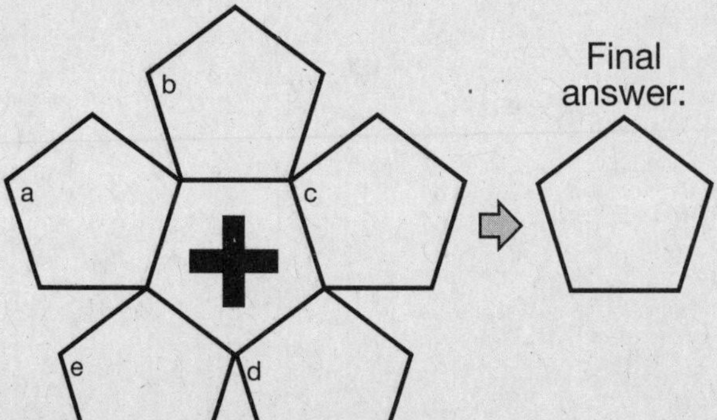

KAKOOMA HARD 5 MULTIPLICATION

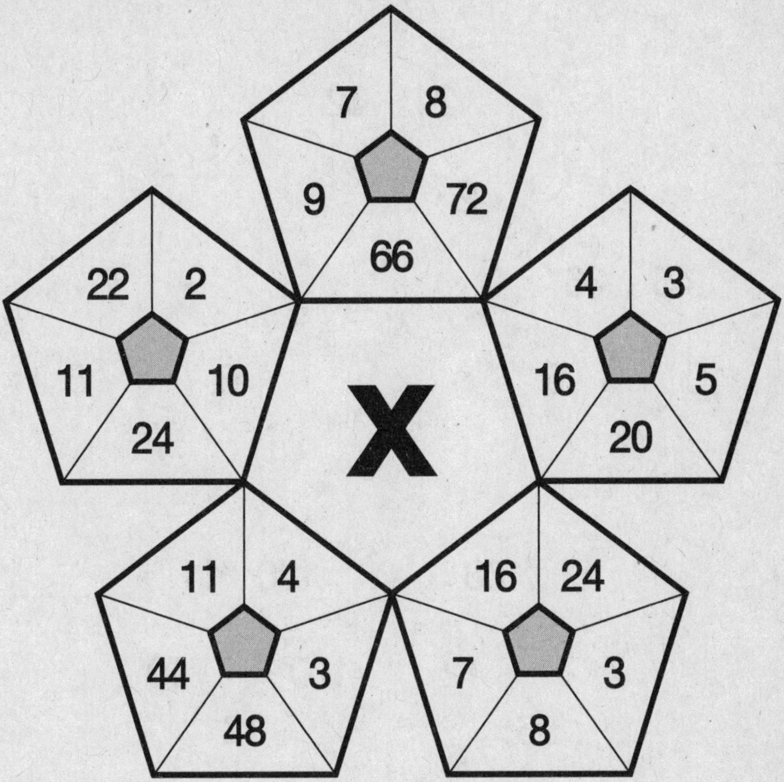

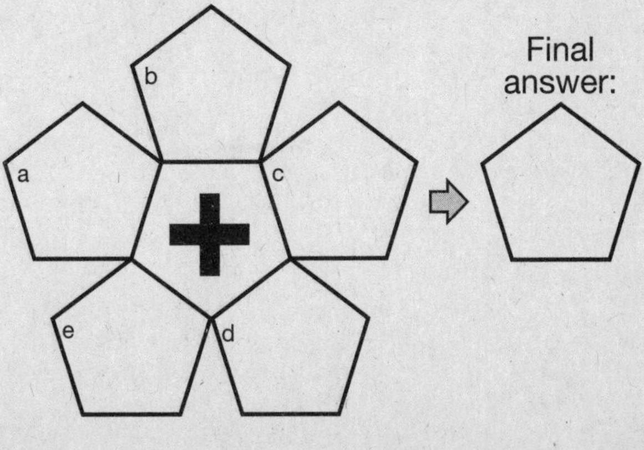

KAKOOMA HARD 5 MULTIPLICATION

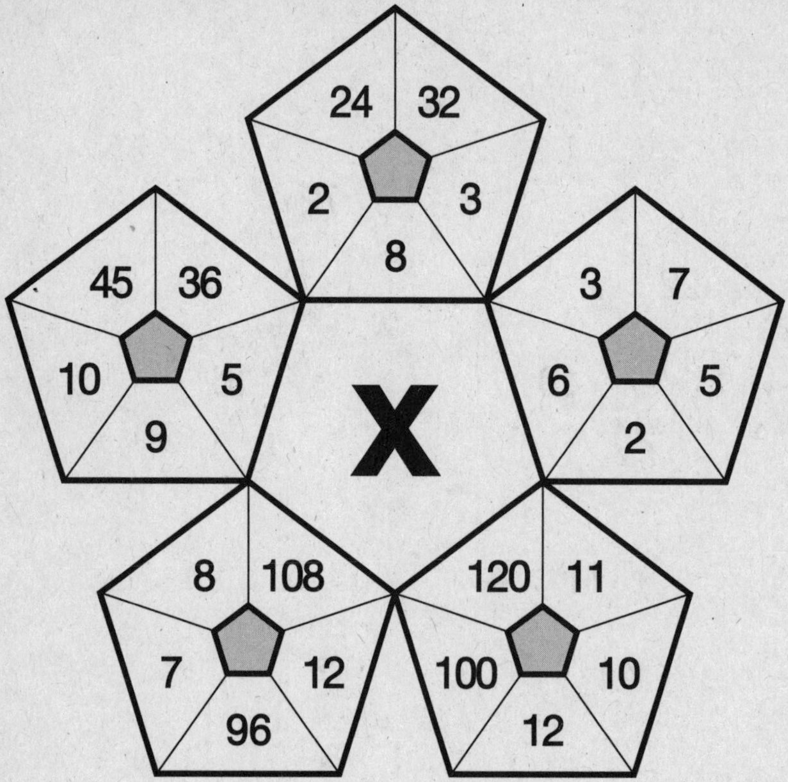

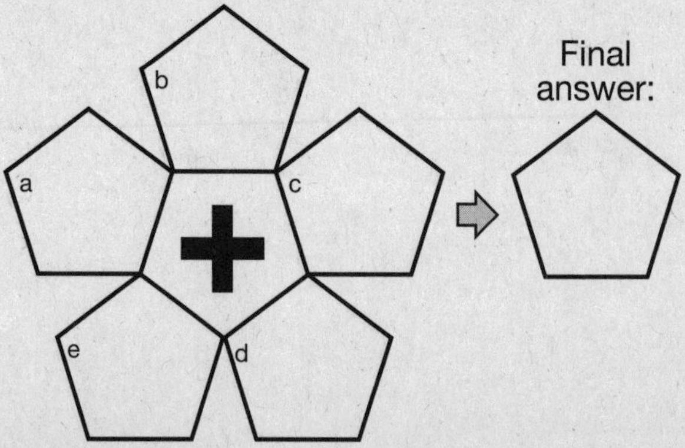

KAKOOMA HARD 5 MULTIPLICATION

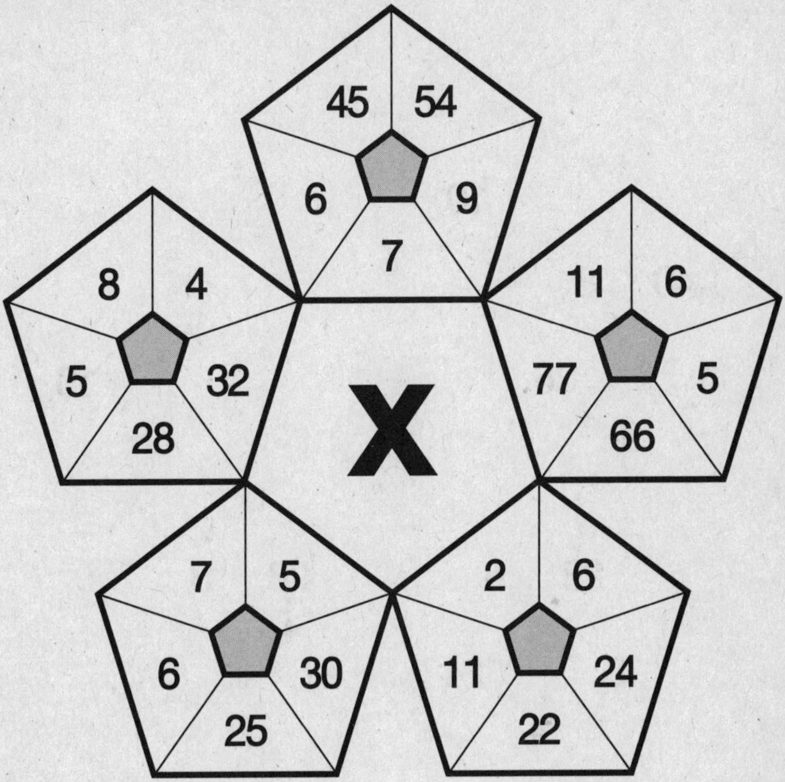

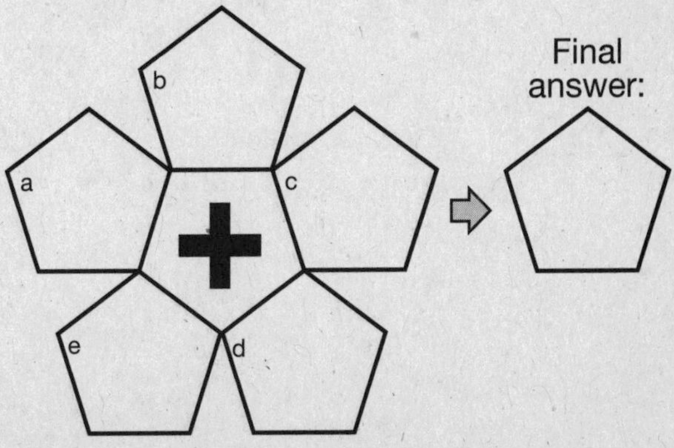

KAKOOMA HARD 5 MULTIPLICATION

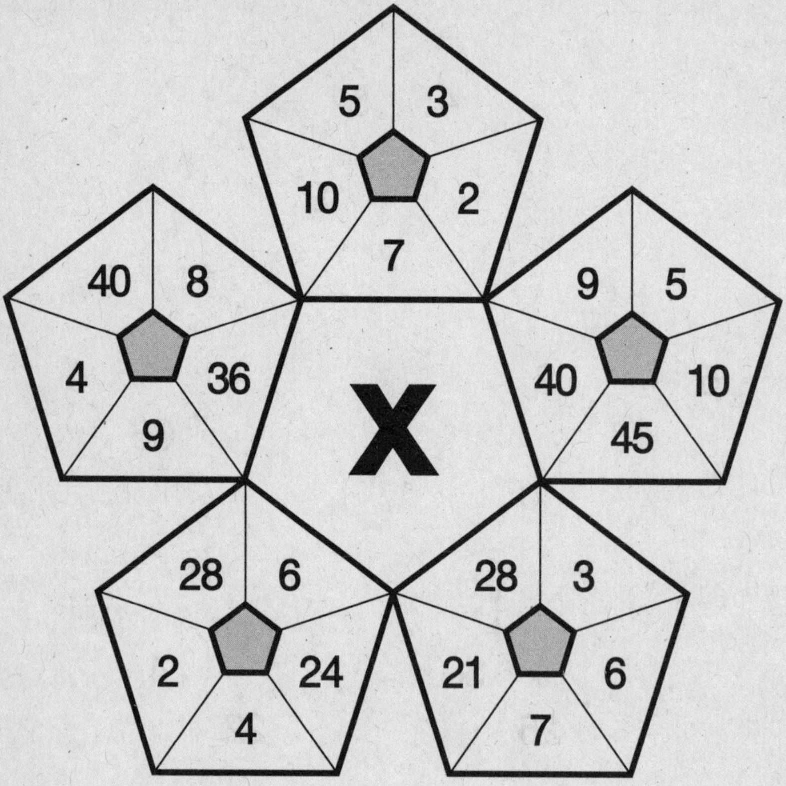

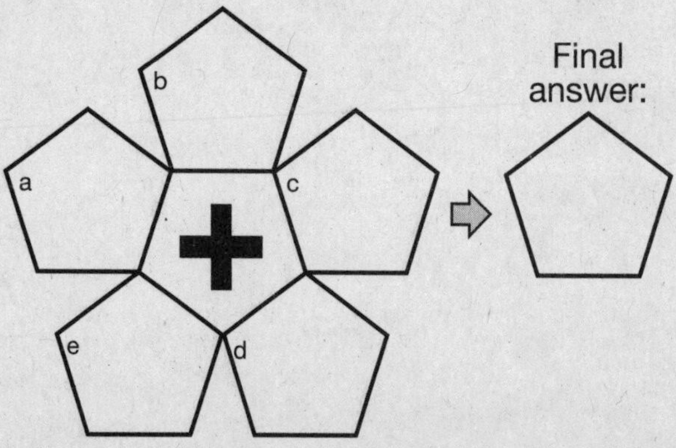

KAKOOMA HARD 6 MULTIPLICATION

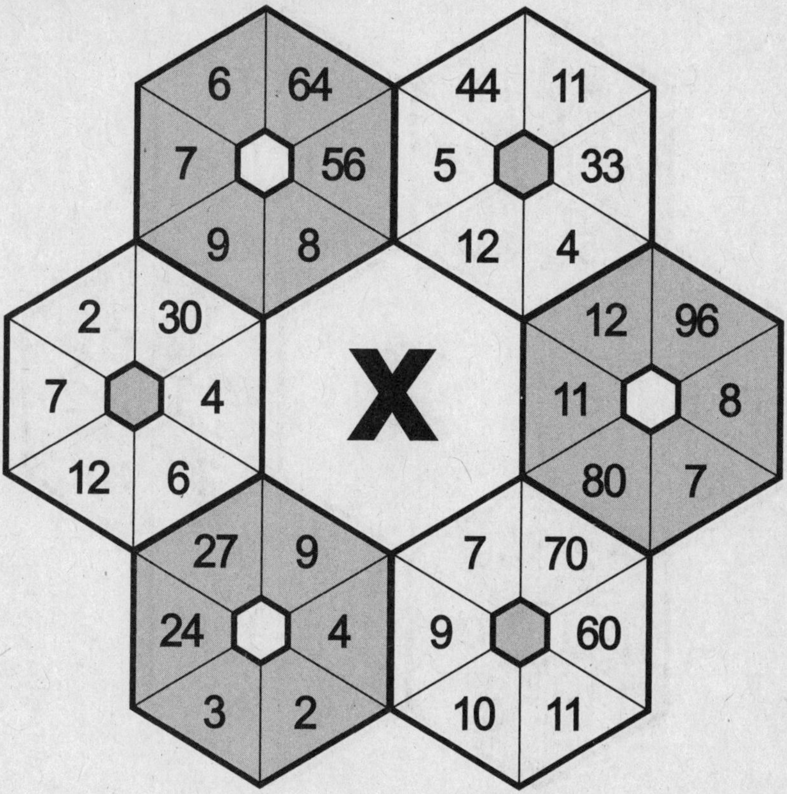

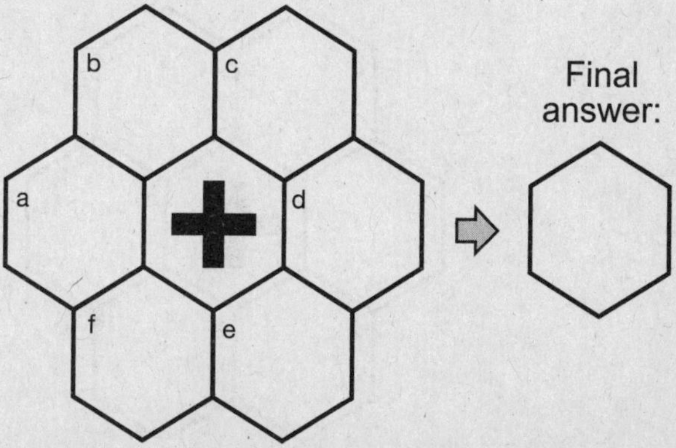

KAKOOMA HARD 6 MULTIPLICATION

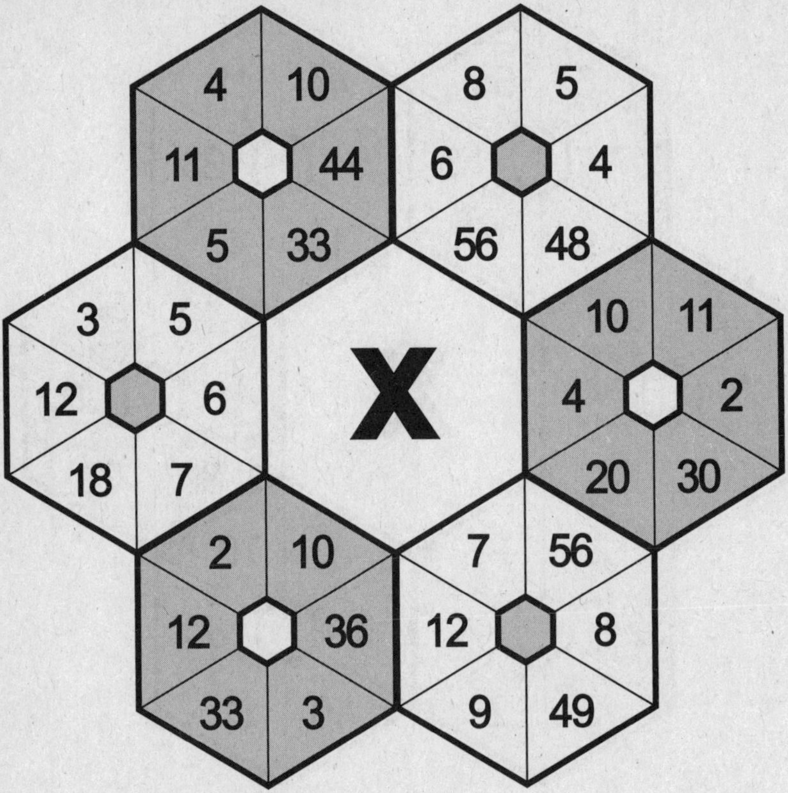

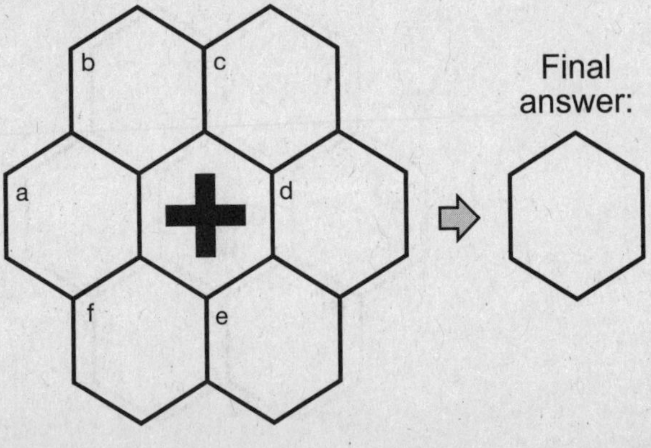

KAKOOMA HARD 6 MULTIPLICATION

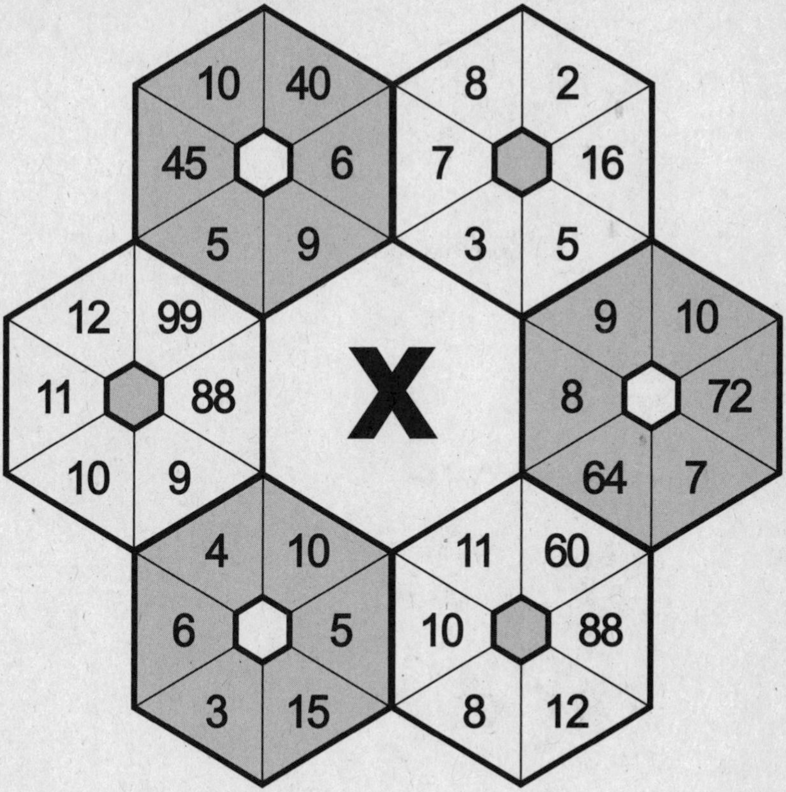

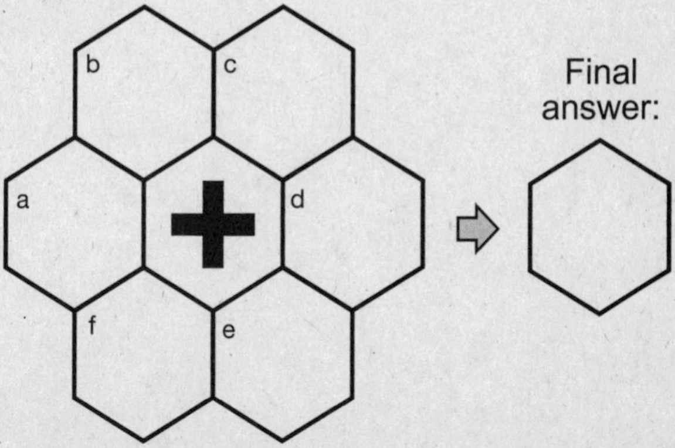

KAKOOMA HARD 6 MULTIPLICATION

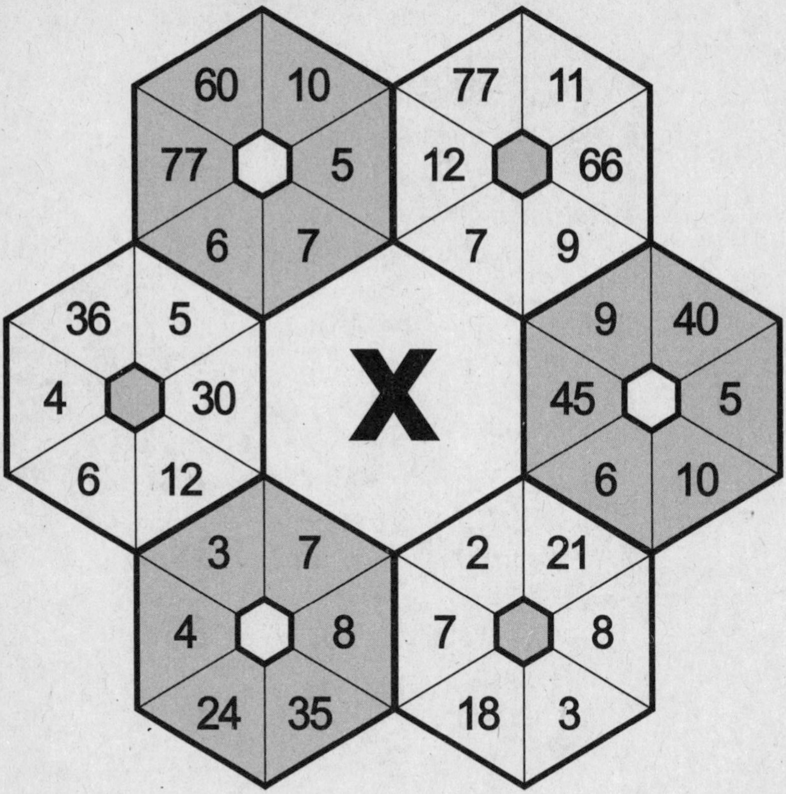

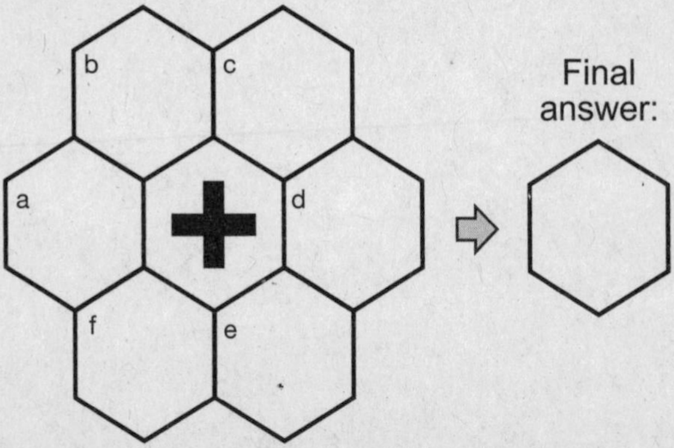

KAKOOMA HARD 6 MULTIPLICATION

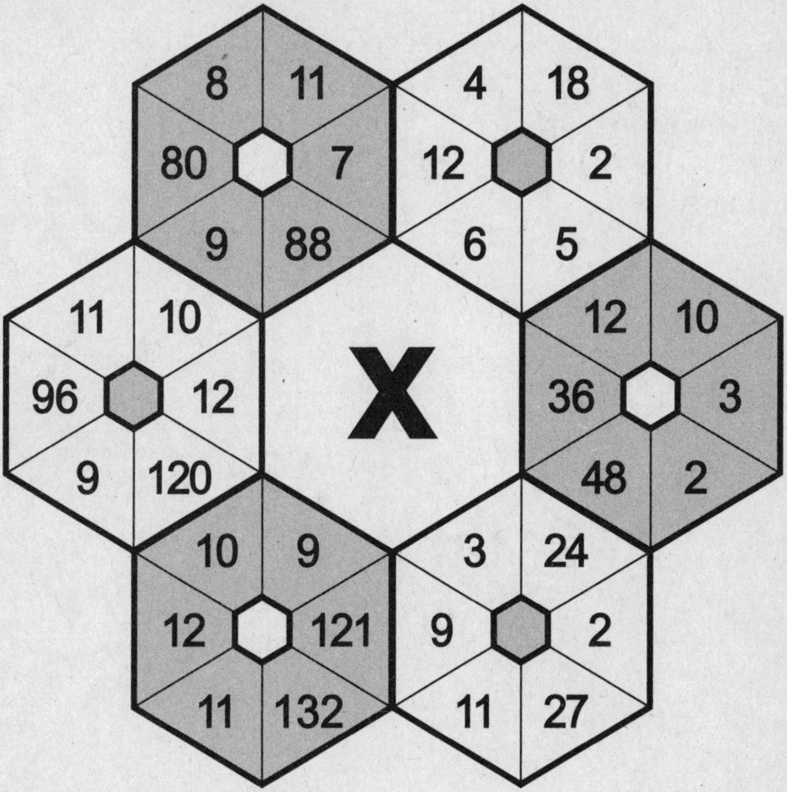

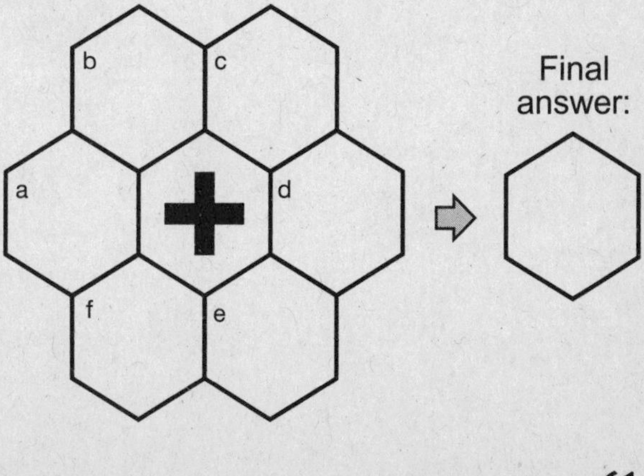

KAKOOMA HARD 6 MULTIPLICATION

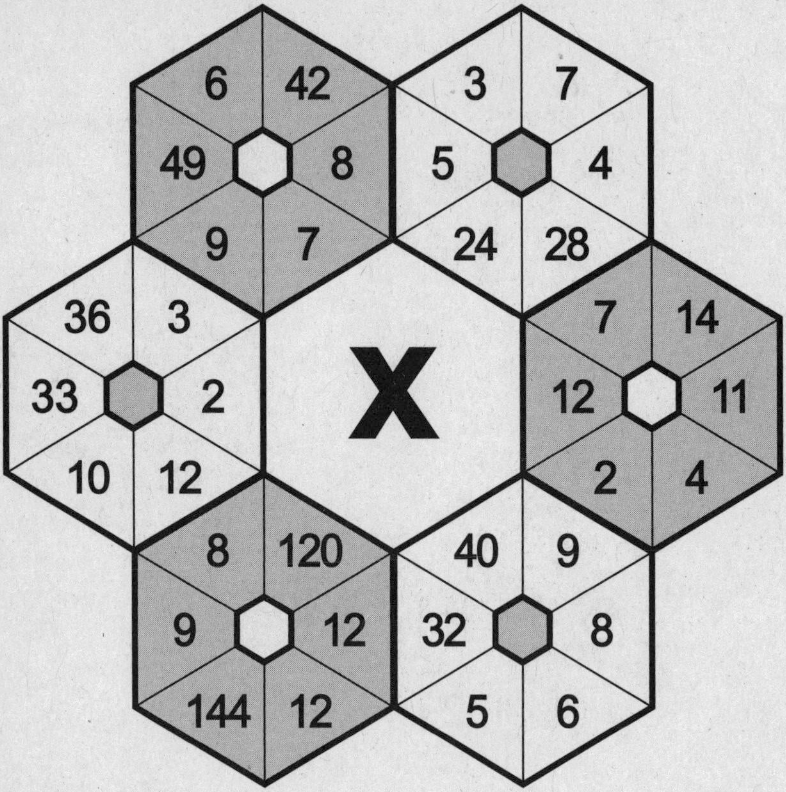

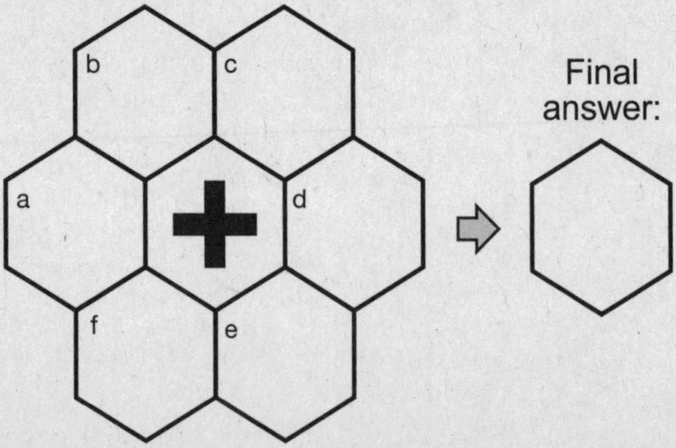

KAKOOMA HARD 6 MULTIPLICATION

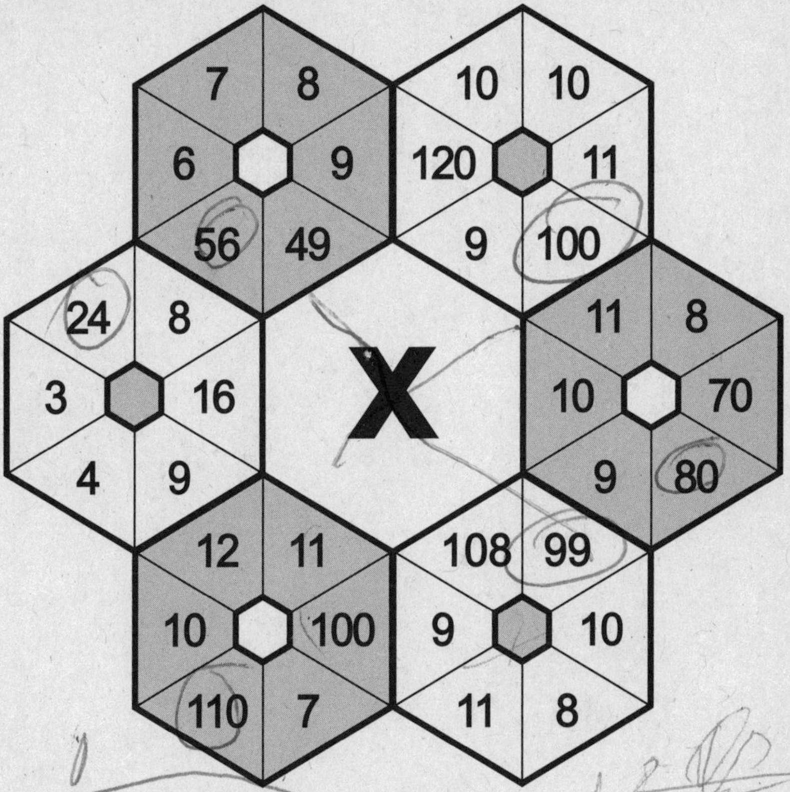

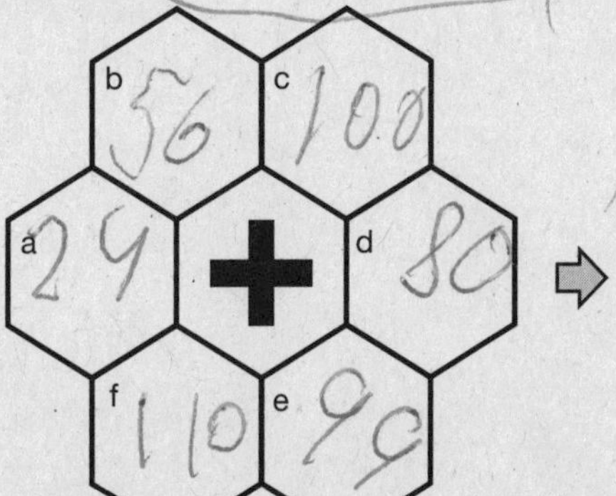

Final answer:

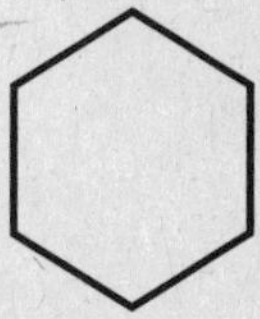

KAKOOMA HARD 6 MULTIPLICATION

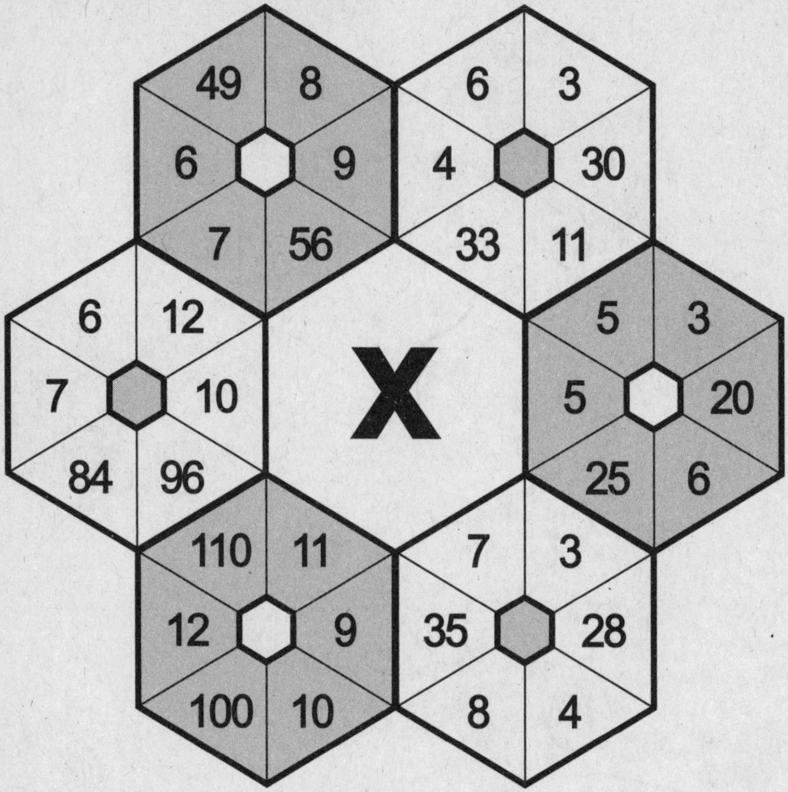

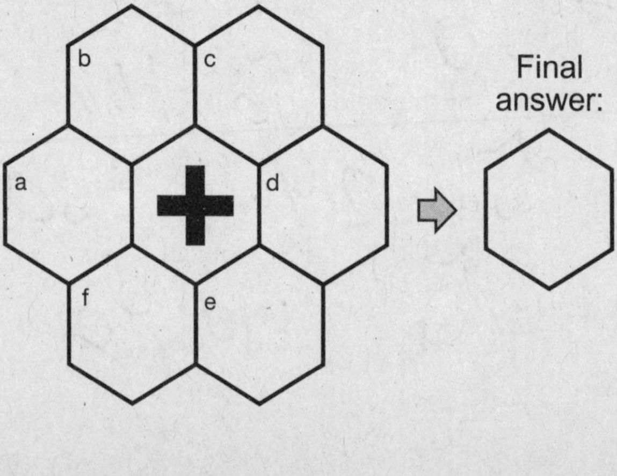

KAKOOMA HARD 6 MULTIPLICATION

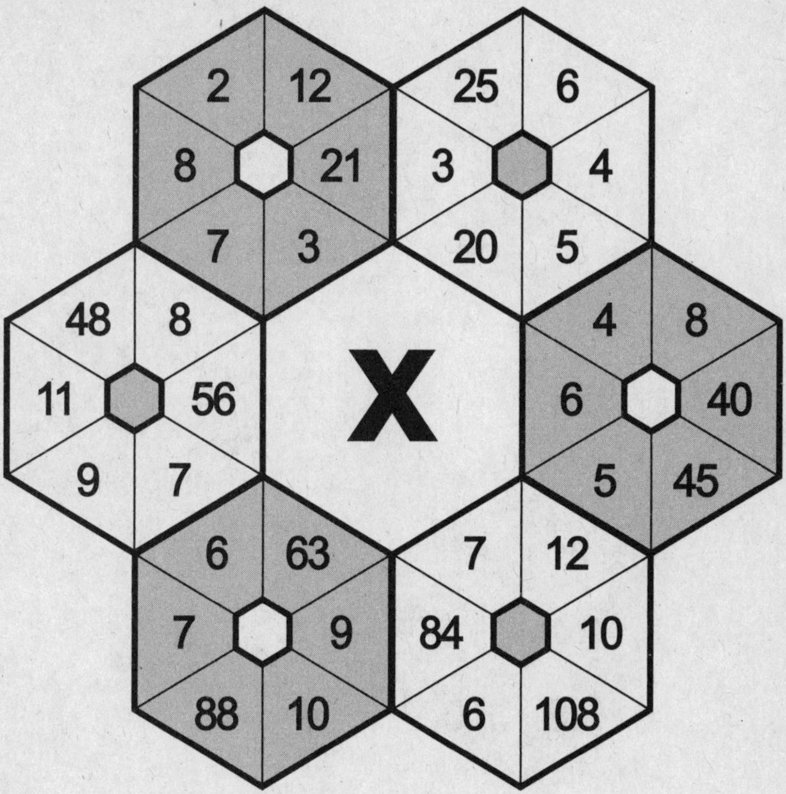

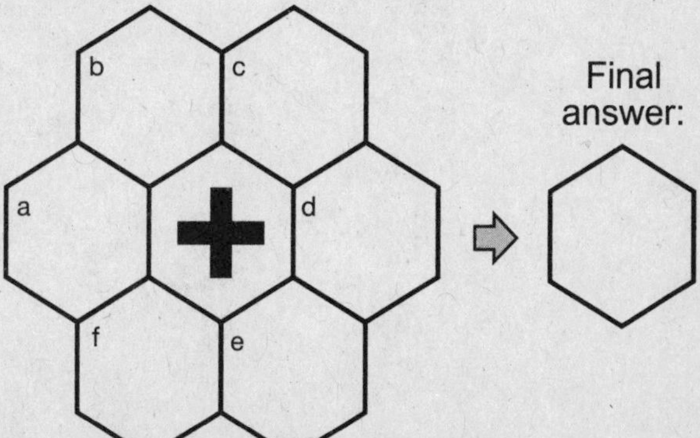

KAKOOMA HARD 6 MULTIPLICATION

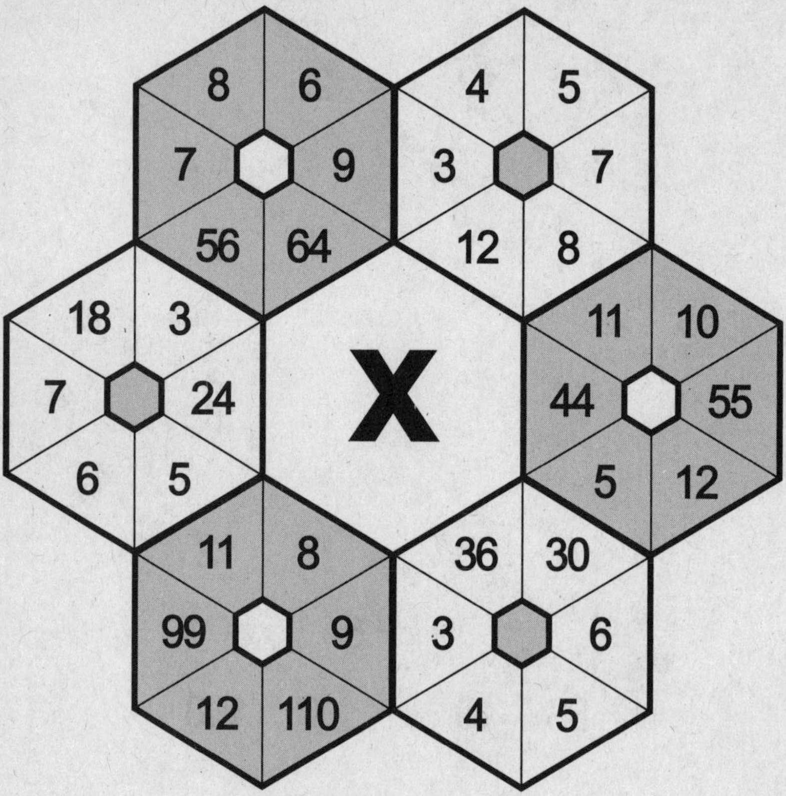

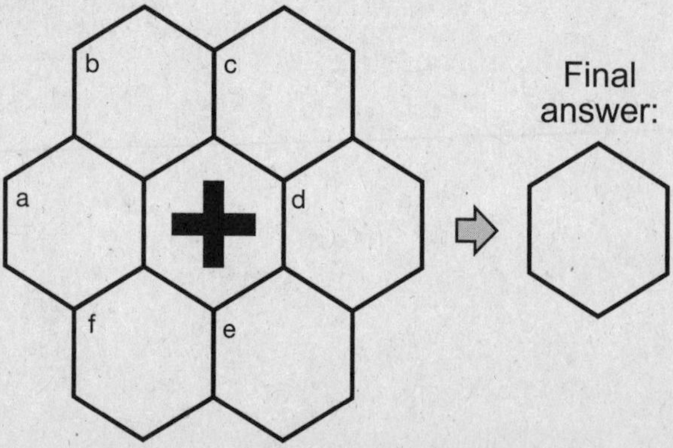

KAKOOMA HARD 6 MULTIPLICATION

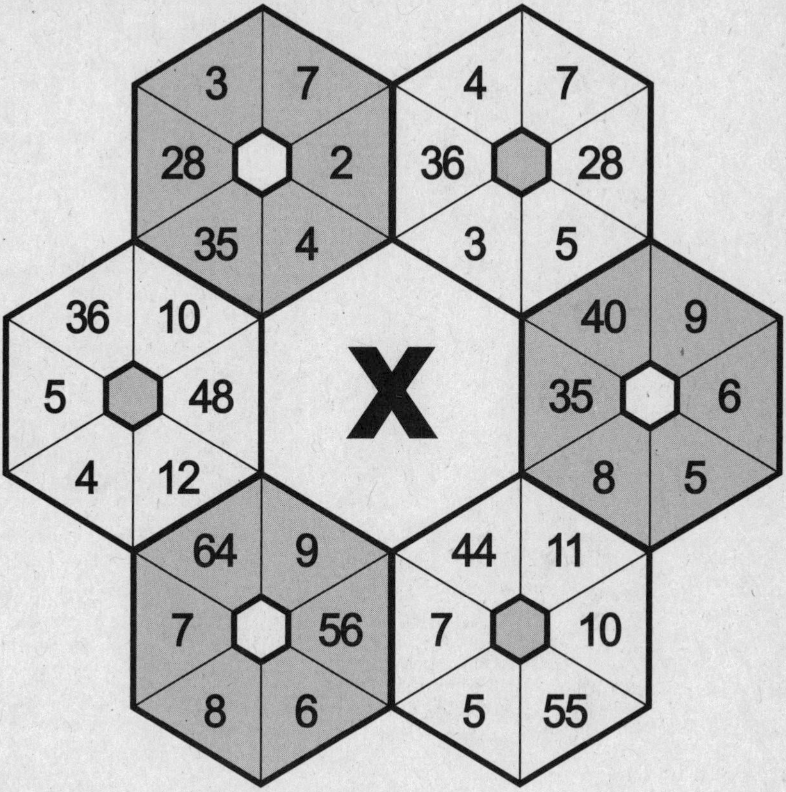

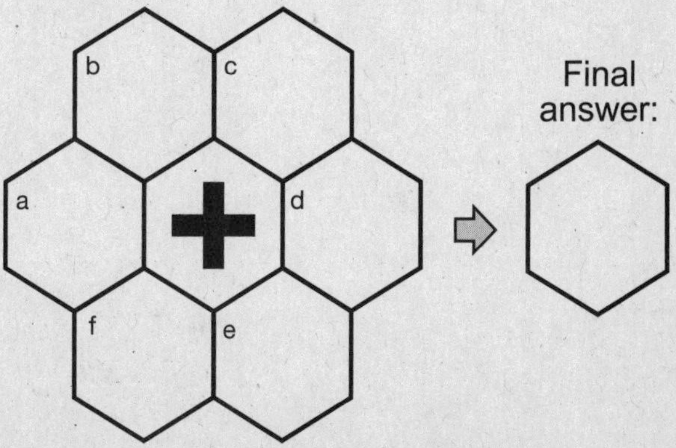

KAKOOMA HARD 6 MULTIPLICATION

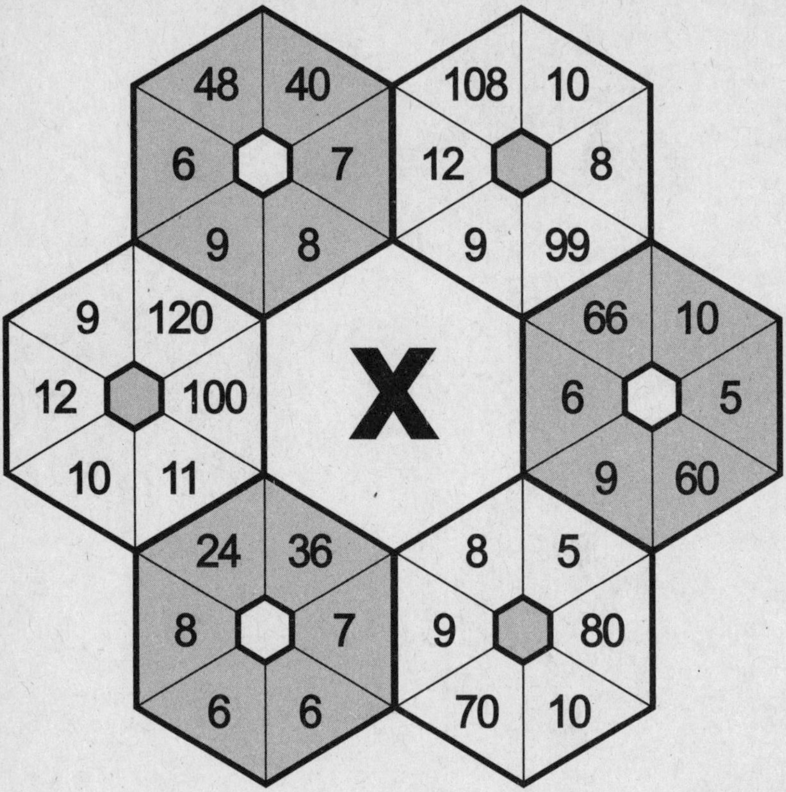

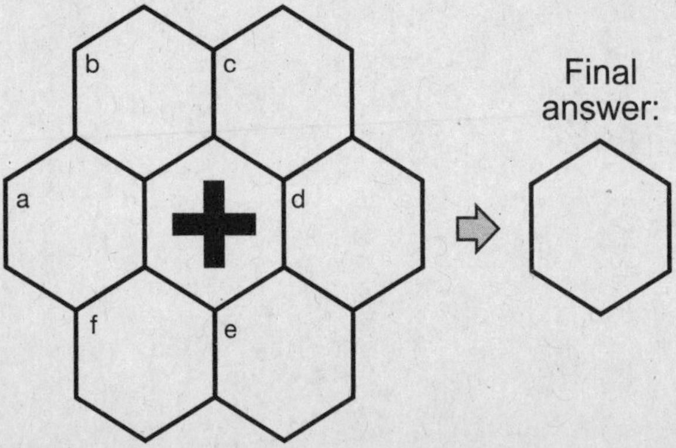

KAKOOMA HARD 6 MULTIPLICATION

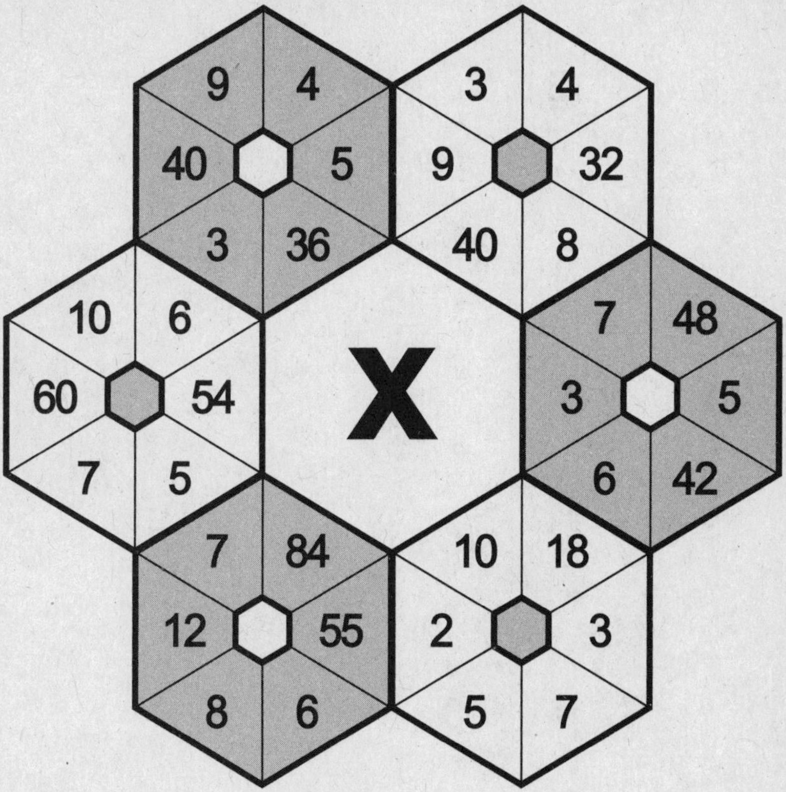

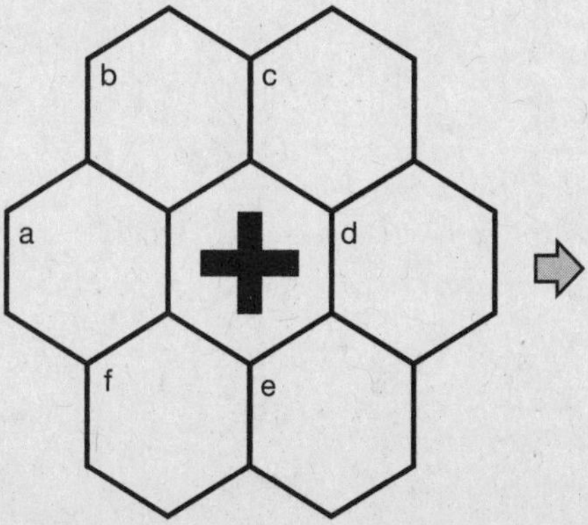

Final answer:

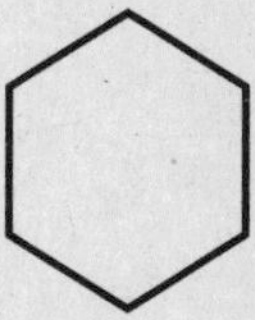

KAKOOMA HARD 6 MULTIPLICATION

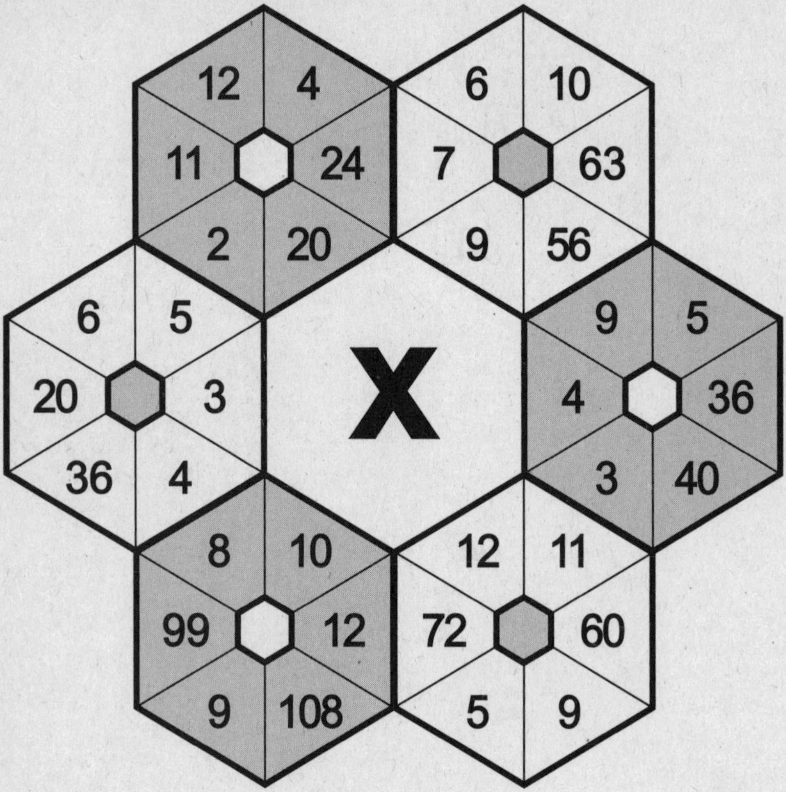

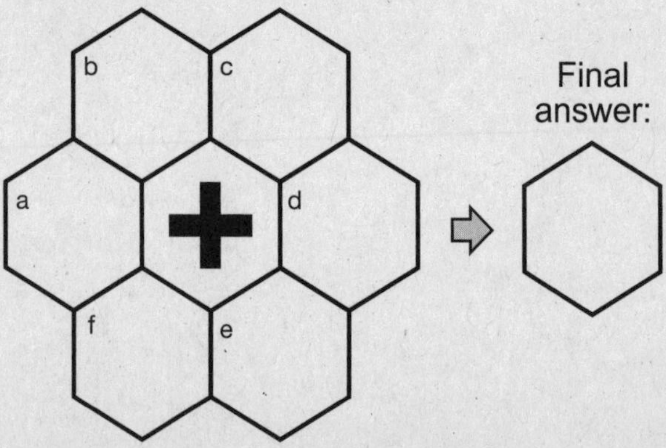

KAKOOMA HARD 6 MULTIPLICATION

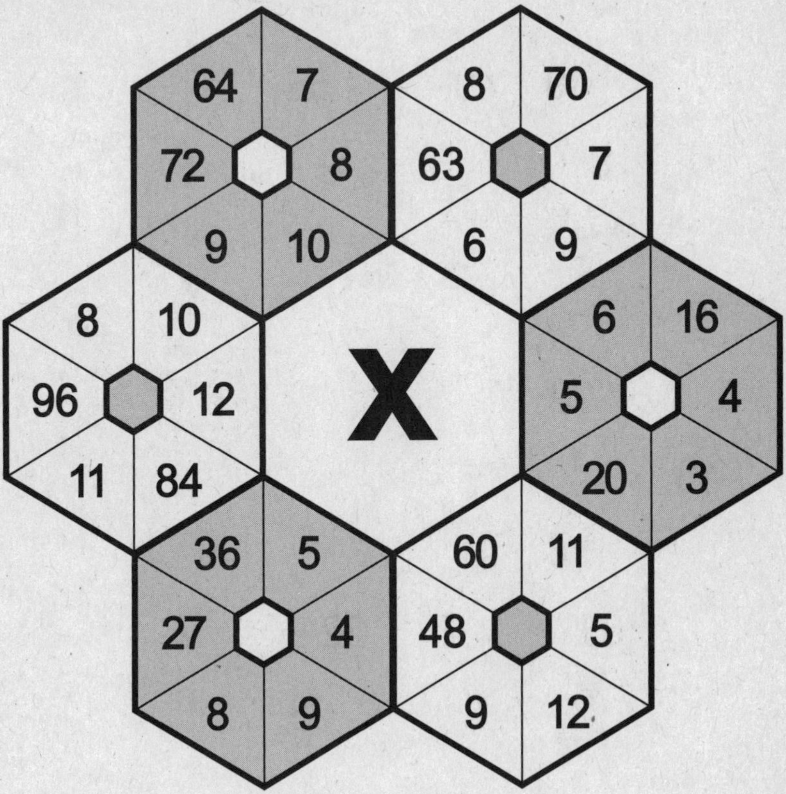

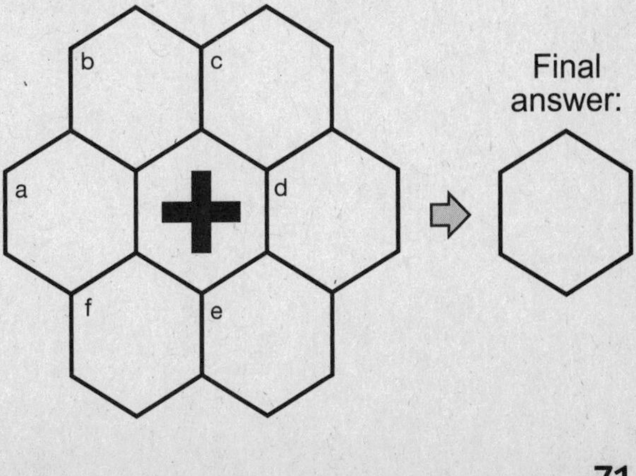

KAKOOMA HARD 6 MULTIPLICATION

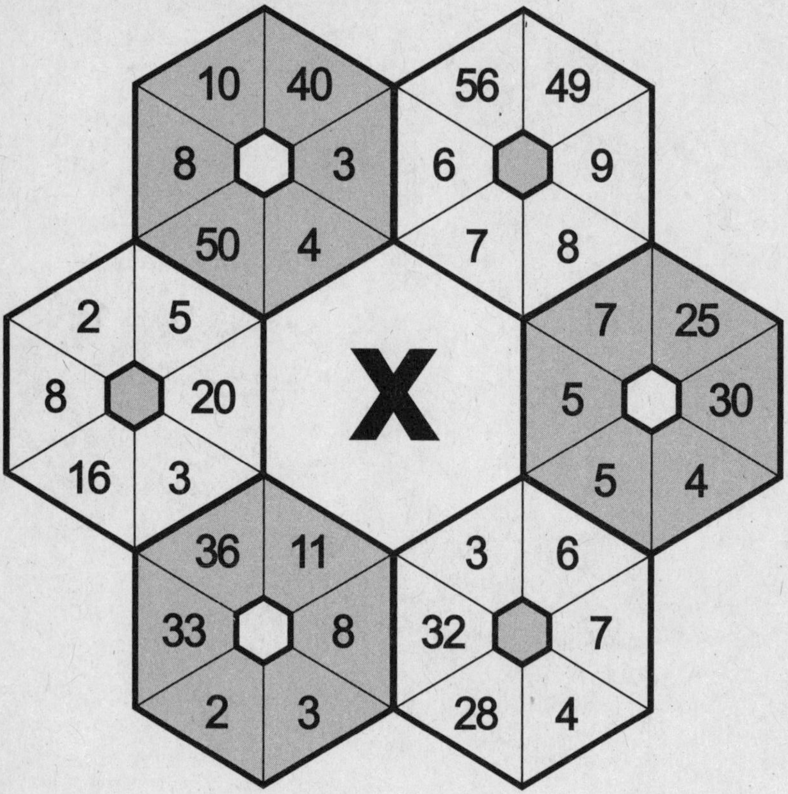

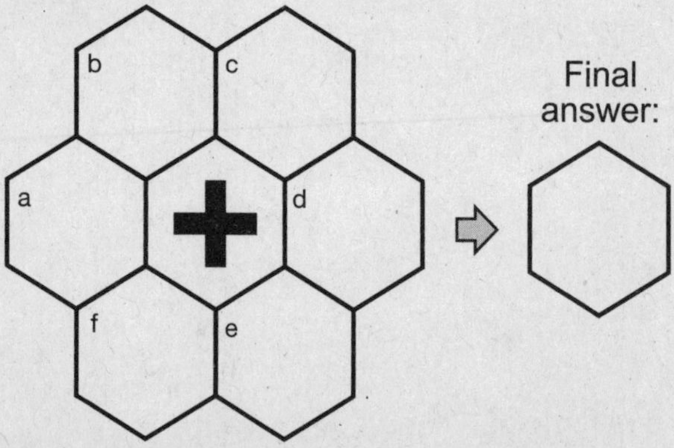

KAKOOMA HARD 6 MULTIPLICATION

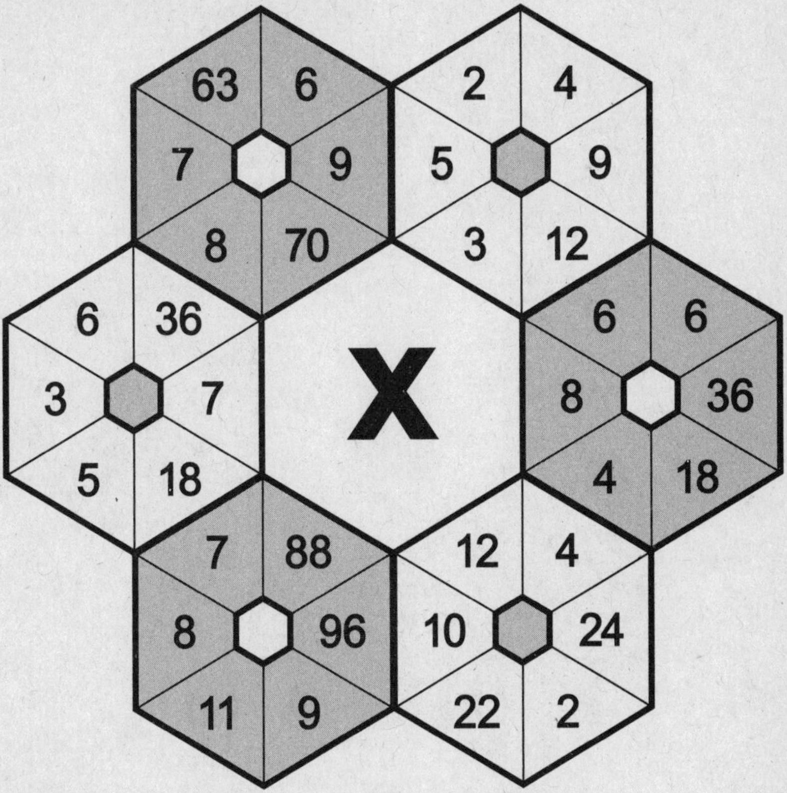

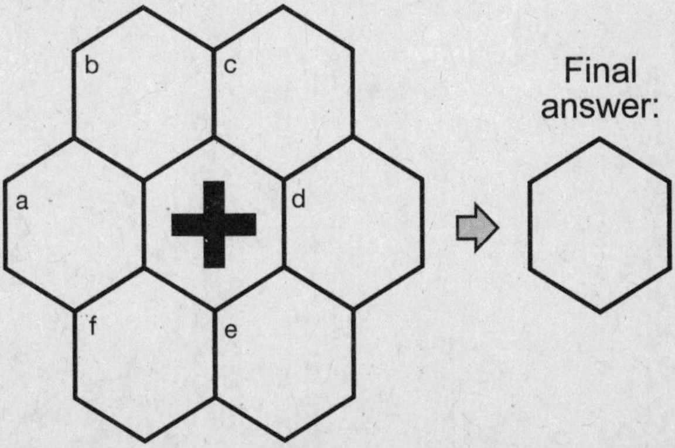

KAKOOMA HARD 6 MULTIPLICATION

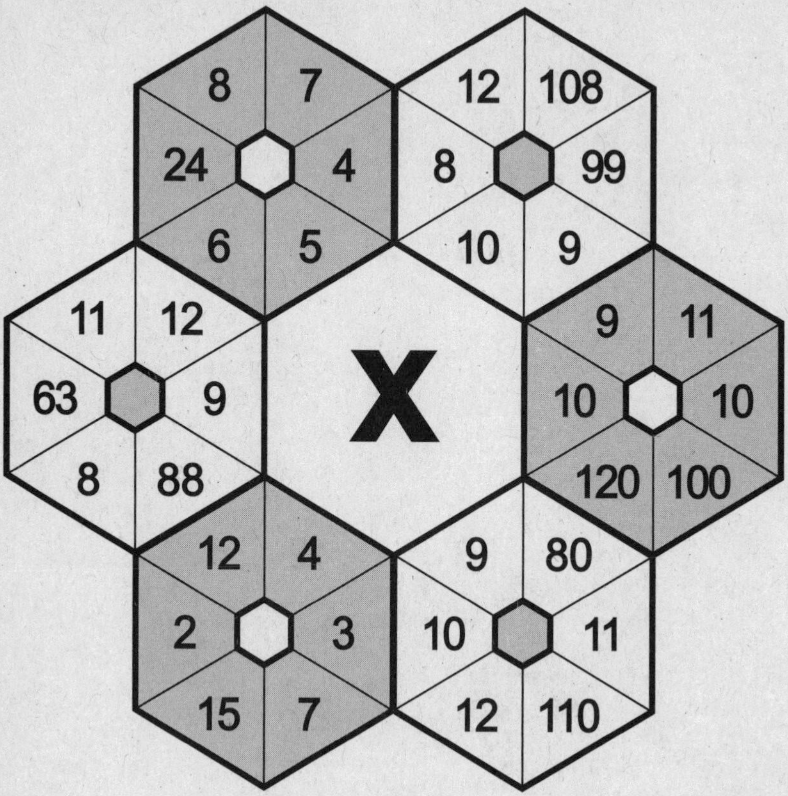

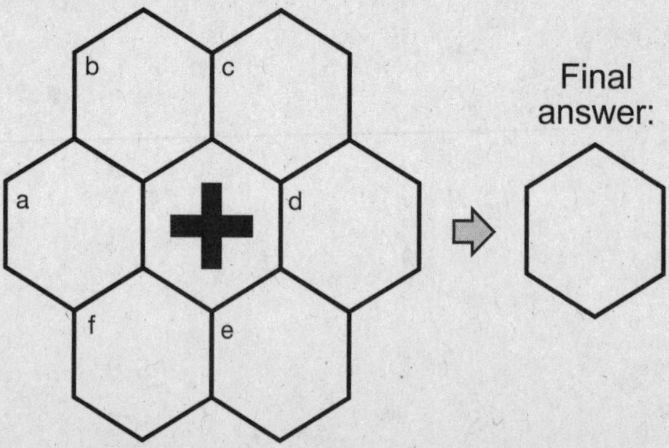

KAKOOMA HARD 6 MULTIPLICATION

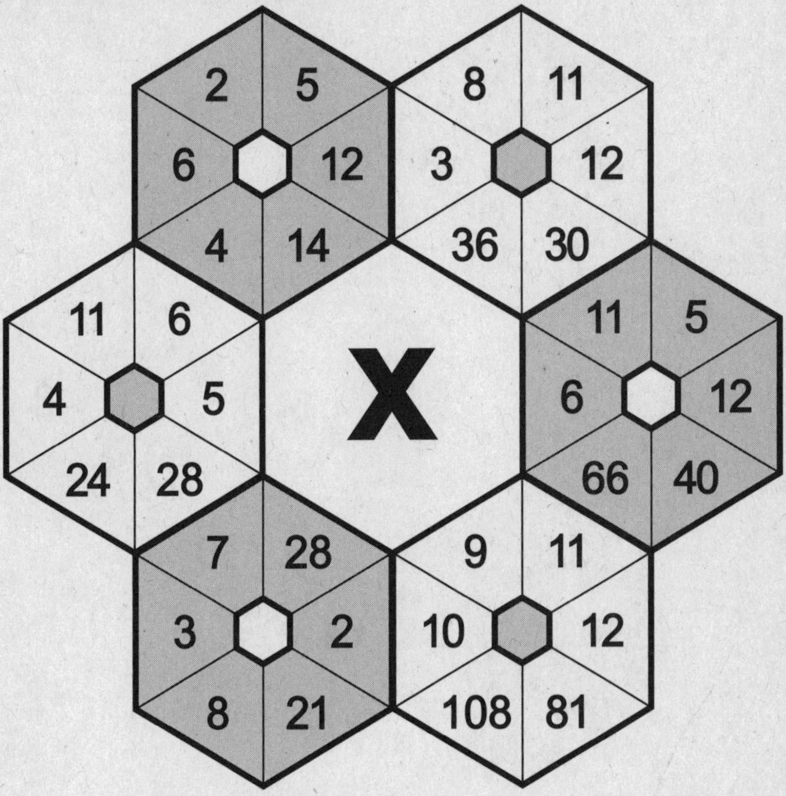

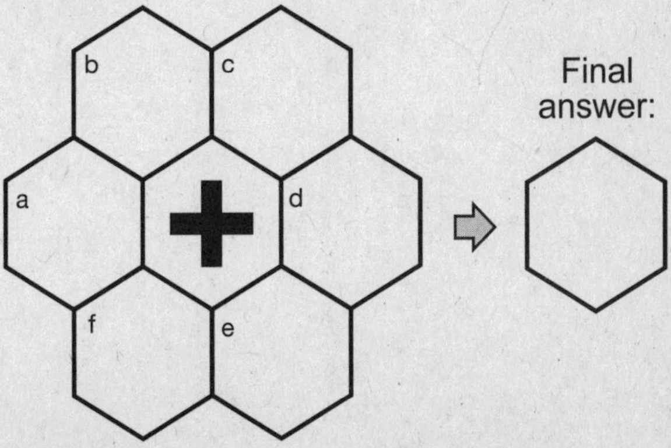

KAKOOMA HARD 6 MULTIPLICATION

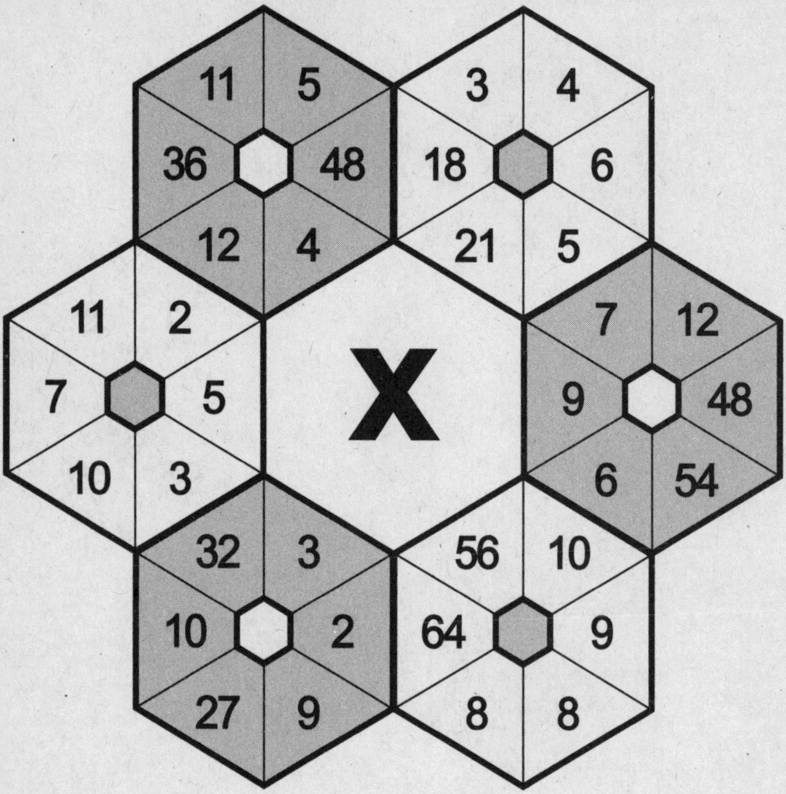

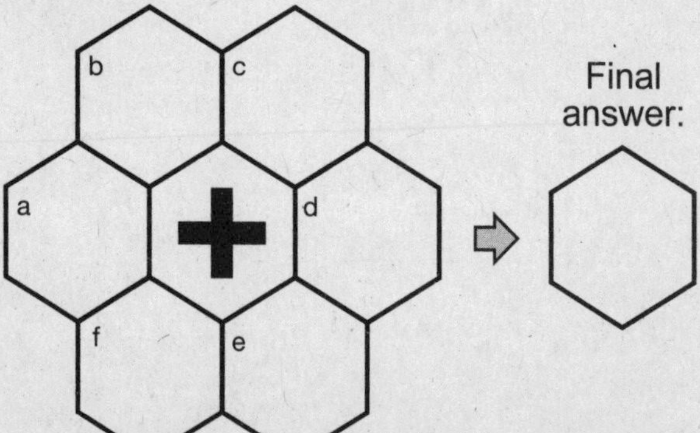

KAKOOMA HARD 6 MULTIPLICATION

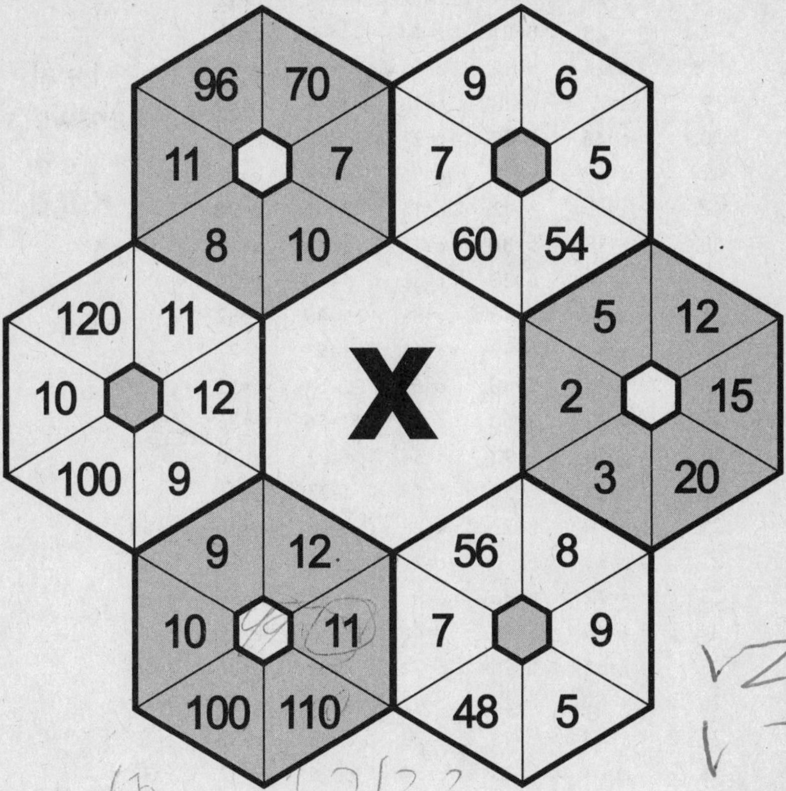

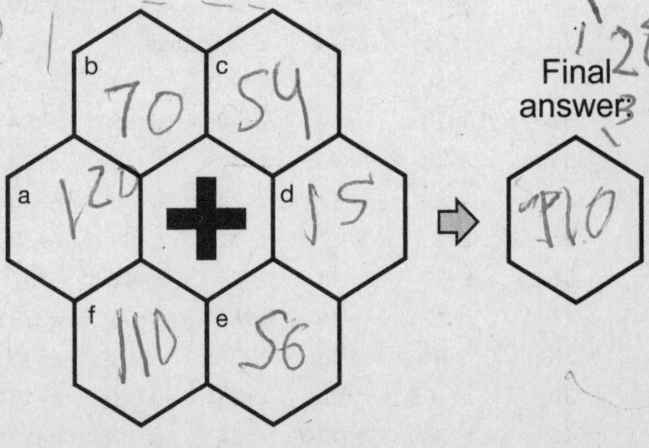

KAKOOMA SOLUTIONS

Final answers are in **BOLD.**

6.	a=**56**	b=24	c=32	d=42	e=12	
7.	a=28	b=21	c=**64**	d=40	e=24	
8.	a=24	b=12	c=16	d=**36**	e=54	
9.	a=72	b=18	c=10	d=24	e=**42**	
10.	a=**48**	b=32	c=27	d=8	e=16	
11.	a=**63**	b=30	c=36	d=48	e=27	
12.	a=63	b=12	c=16	d=18	e=**28**	
13.	a=18	b=**36**	c=45	d=24	e=18	
14.	a=20	b=28	c=36	d=**48**	e=21	
15.	a=12	b=36	c=81	d=**48**	e=32	
16.	a=6	b=49	c=14	d=**63**	e=27	
17.	a=16	b=**48**	c=63	d=70	e=32	
18.	a=32	b=60	c=20	d=**56**	e=36	
19.	a=16	b=**72**	c=56	d=32	e=70	
20.	a=28	b=50	c=**63**	d=27	e=35	
21.	a=70	b=27	c=28	d=36	e=20	f=**63**
22.	a=30	b=70	c=27	d=20	e=54	f=**81**
23.	a=**72**	b=30	c=8	d=36	e=36	f=56
24.	a=36	b=63	c=**48**	d=40	e=18	f=12
25.	a=32	b=56	c=**72**	d=63	e=30	f=16
26.	a=**60**	b=28	c=42	d=18	e=48	f=4
27.	a=**64**	b=42	c=20	d=48	e=35	f=16
28.	a=24	b=21	c=**50**	d=18	e=12	f=32
29.	a=21	b=80	c=**54**	d=24	e=30	f=32
30.	a=36	b=24	c=54	d=49	e=8	f=**60**
31.	a=30	b=**54**	c=24	d=42	e=36	f=9
32.	a=24	b=54	c=40	d=36	e=**64**	f=80
33.	a=18	b=**45**	c=42	d=40	e=27	f=6
34.	a=24	b=12	c=72	d=56	e=30	f=**54**
35.	a=18	b=27	c=**72**	d=8	e=30	f=64
36.	a=30	b=14	c=18	d=**36**	e=22	
37.	a=**121**	b=16	c=88	d=66	e=33	
38.	a=**48**	b=10	c=28	d=63	e=20	
39.	a=108	b=24	c=54	d=18	e=**132**	
40.	a=36	b=**120**	c=84	d=108	e=110	
41.	a=110	b=27	c=**55**	d=48	e=28	

KAKOOMA SOLUTIONS

42.	a=45	b=32	c=10	d=72	e=**77**	
43.	a=12	b=44	c=30	d=**42**	e=35	
44.	a=60	b=40	c=72	d=36	e=**96**	
45.	a=**84**	b=16	c=60	d=24	e=54	
46.	a=27	b=8	c=**64**	d=40	e=24	
47.	a=18	b=54	c=**72**	d=77	e=27	
48.	a=**54**	b=21	c=18	d=36	e=8	
49.	a=63	b=**44**	c=12	d=32	e=30	
50.	a=24	b=40	c=36	d=32	e=**72**	
51.	a=120	b=66	c=36	d=44	e=**80**	
52.	a=21	b=96	c=45	d=**49**	e=28	
53.	a=22	b=72	c=20	d=24	e=**44**	
54.	a=45	b=24	c=6	d=**120**	e=96	
55.	a=32	b=**54**	c=66	d=22	e=30	
56.	a=36	b=10	c=**45**	d=21	e=24	
57.	a=12	b=**56**	c=44	d=96	e=70	f=27
58.	a=18	b=44	c=48	d=20	e=**56**	f=36
59.	a=99	b=45	c=16	d=72	e=**88**	f=15
60.	a=30	b=60	c=77	d=**45**	e=21	f=24
61.	a=120	b=88	c=12	d=36	e=27	f=**132**
62.	a=36	b=**42**	c=28	d=14	e=40	f=144
63.	a=24	b=56	c=100	d=**80**	e=99	f=110
64.	a=**84**	b=56	c=33	d=25	e=28	f=110
65.	a=56	b=21	c=20	d=40	e=**84**	f=63
66.	a=18	b=56	c=12	d=55	e=**30**	f=99
67.	a=48	b=28	c=28	d=40	e=55	f=**56**
68.	a=120	b=48	c=**108**	d=60	e=80	f=36
69.	a=60	b=36	c=32	d=**42**	e=10	f=84
70.	a=20	b=24	c=63	d=36	e=**60**	f=108
71.	a=**96**	b=72	c=63	d=20	e=60	f=36
72.	a=16	b=40	c=**56**	d=25	e=28	f=33
73.	a=18	b=63	c=12	d=**36**	e=24	f=88
74.	a=88	b=24	c=108	d=**100**	e=110	f=12
75.	a=24	b=12	c=**36**	d=66	e=108	f=21
76.	a=10	b=48	c=18	d=54	e=**64**	f=27
77.	a=120	b=70	c=54	d=15	e=56	f=**110**

Congratulations—you solved all the puzzles in this book!
ADD-ICTED TO KAKOOMA?
More good times lay ahead!
KAKOOMA
LET'S PLAY AT KAKOOMA.COM